Catholicism for the Non-Catholic

Catholicism for the Non-Catholic

A Brief Introduction to
Catholic Christianity

by
The Reverend Richard Chiola, Ph.D.

Templegate Publishers
Springfield, Illinois

Published by
Templegate Publishers, LLC
302 East Adams Street
Post Office Box 5152
Springfield, Illinois
62701-5152
217-522-3353
templegate.com

Copyright © 2006 Richard Chiola
ISBN 13: 978-0-87243-269-7
ISBN 10: 0-87243-269-6
Library of Congress Control Number 2006907988

Without limiting the rights under copyright reserved above, no part of this publication may be reproduced, stored in or introduced into a retrieval system, or transmitted, in any form, or by any means (electronic, mechanical, photocopying, recording, or otherwise), without the prior written permission of the above publisher of this book.

Printed and bound in the United States of America
by Publishers' Graphics, LLC

This book is dedicated to
Sr. Pauletta Overbeck,
a Springfield Dominican,
teacher and spiritual mentor.

Contents

Acknowledgements	9
Chapter 1	
An Overview	11
Chapter 2	
The Continuity of Faith	27
Chapter 3	
Authority in the Church	47
Chapter 4	
The Protestant Reformation	81
Chapter 5	
The Second Vatican Council	103
Chapter 6	
The Uniqueness of the Church	115
Chapter 7	
Prayer	135
Chapter 8	
The Communion of Saints	169
Appendix	185
Bibliography	191

Acknowledgements

The author appreciates the assistance of Dr. Susan Karina Dickey, O.P., the Reverend John Nolan, and Ed Renier who read and corrected the text. Their help and encouragement was invaluable.

The biblical quotations are excerpts from the *New American Bible,* Confraternity of Christian Doctrine, Washington, D.C., 1970). Quotations from the early Christian writers and other Catholic spiritual writers are from the *Liturgy of the Hours* (International Committee on English in the Liturgy, 1975). Quotations from the documents of the Second Vatican Council are taken from *Vatican Council II: the Conciliar and Post Conciliar Documents* (Ed., Austin Flannery, O.P., Costello Publishing Co., Northport, New York, 1975). The "Glory to God" and Eucharistic Prayer II in the Appendix are taken from the *Sacramentary* (International Committee on English in the Liturgy, 1973).

1
An Overview

The number of disciples of Jesus of Nazareth at the time of his death in the year 33 is not known. We do know they included both men and women drawn from the various branches of Judaism and represented diverse economic and social groups. Their diversity is attested repeatedly in the written accounts called the Christian Scriptures or New Testament. Diversity is one of the defining qualities of local churches that grew up in witness to his resurrection from the dead. The Greek term *catholicos*, meaning inclusively universal, designates a church diverse in its membership. In this sense "a Catholic" describes universal inclusion in a particular church of all the diverse economic, social and racial groups within a specific locale. Such a church, under the authority of a bishop and often called a diocese, is a Catholic Church. However, Catholic is most often used in another way, to describe the communion of all these Churches with the Church of Rome. As such, Catholic means inclusion of all the local or particular Churches throughout the world in one universal or Catholic Church. This Catholic Church, however, has more than one dynamic manifestation. There is the Roman or western Church and the eastern Churches which are either Oriental or Byzantine. While the number of his followers in 33 A.D. is unknown, the number of those who claim Jesus as the source of their life and unity in the Catholic Church currently numbers about one fifth of the human race.

The Catholic Church traces its origin to Jesus, Latin for the Hebrew *Yeshua* (or in English *Joshua*). He is called "the Christ," a Greek equivalent of the Hebrew *messiah* or anointed one of God. This Jesus was crucified by the local Roman authorities outside the city of Jerusalem at about forty years of age. He was a Jew. His preaching was summed up by his followers as, "Repent and believe the Good News." The theme of repentance was preached by other Jewish holy men of his time. In Christ's proclamation, repentance is a complete change of life. It is based on faith in God and manifest in specific life practices that reflect the Kingdom of God already breaking into the world.

Some Jews called for revolt from the oppression of Roman occupation of their land. Jesus did not. Rather, he called for repentance to usher in the Kingdom of God. Though not a kingdom of this world, it was manifested in this world by the love of enemies and care for the poor and the outcast. At the end of this world, his kingdom would come in fullness and bring resurrection of the body and eternal life. The way to this kingdom was faith in the Good News he preached. "Good News" is the translation of another Greek word now rendered as Gospel but in Old English as *Godspel*. The Good News is that the Son of God was sent into this world to lay down his life in order to bring a new world into being, a world sustained by the fullness of God's life and love. Christ's followers proclaimed their faith that God's Kingdom had come through the death and resurrection of Jesus rather than a violent change in government.

The original disciples of Jesus were Jews, a loose community, called the Way, and initially appeared to be one of several Jewish sects. Very quickly they became known as Christians. Almost as quickly Christians were persecuted for proclaiming that Jesus was the Christ sent by the God of Israel, who raised him from the dead and by doing so showed him to be Son of God and Lord of all. His followers declared that they shared his Spirit, sent from his Father. Christ commissioned them to baptize everyone who accepted this Good News into the life of the Father and the Son and the Holy Spirit. They were to prepare the world for Christ to come again at the end of time to gather every creature to God as the Father of all.

Jewish sects practiced ritual washings on a number of occasions. One notable sect followed John, called the Baptist. He received the name "the Baptist" because his call for repentance culminated in a ritual washing. Christians call John the Forerunner because he was sent by God to prepare the way for the coming of the Christ. John baptized Jesus at the beginning of his public ministry. The followers of Jesus also practiced ritual washing or "baptism" from the Greek Word meaning "to go down." Specifically it meant to go down into the water but more importantly to go down by faith into the death of Jesus, enter his resurrection, and share in his divine life with the Father and the Holy Spirit.

The proclamation that Jesus is the Son of God was the breaking point with Judaism. Christians were cast out of the synagogues, persecuted by Jewish leaders and became a separate synagogue or gathering of the People of God. This gathering was rendered *synaxis* in Greek, *ecclesia* in Latin, and as *church* in English. Membership in the Catholic Church was through faith in the Gospel and baptism in the name of the Father and the Son and the Holy Spirit. Baptism was completed by Confirmation and sharing in the Eucharist, the Body and Blood of the risen Jesus. Catholic Christians were gathered by these sacraments into a new communion of life which is a sharing in the life of God.

During his earthly ministry Jesus initiated some kind of rudimentary structures among his original followers. These structures are attested by the Christian Scriptures. Jesus chose twelve men called the Twelve and sometimes called Apostles. After his resurrection some Apostles exercised authority over the community of his followers at Jerusalem. Others of the Twelve are not referred to again in the Scriptures but are recalled in various Christian traditions as founders of local Churches. The Catholic Churches claim their bishops are successors to the Apostles and that the bishop of Rome, or "Pope," is the successor to Peter as leader of the Twelve. While Jesus initiated structures among his followers, he also initiated relationships that did not depend on these structures. For instance, the Apostles were Christ's chosen witnesses to his resurrection, though not the only ones. Various disciples of Jesus were also witnesses. Some were women, most notably Mary from Magdala, a town in Galilee. Mary stood at his cross during his passion and death. She is famous for being the first to see the risen Christ. The risen Jesus sent her to announce his resurrection to Peter and the other Apostles who had abandoned him in his sufferings. Christ's choice of Mary was a gift to her, a *charism*. His choice of Mary as the Apostle to the Apostles was a charism but not a permanent structure. The Catholic Churches believed Christ's choice of the Twelve was both a gift to them and a permanent structure in the Church.

Through his personal relationship with his disciples, Christ continued after his resurrection to give such charisms, even to this day. Both the structures and the charisms in the Church are the work of the Spirit he promised his disciples he would send after his resurrection. The Spirit sent from Christ's Father, also called the

Holy Spirit and the Spirit of God, created unity among the members of the Church through the tension between these permanent charismatic structures and the personal non-structural charisms.

If there is one person who gathered in himself the various tensions, structures, and charisms of first century Christianity, it was a tentmaker from Tarsus. His Hebrew name is Saul but like many Jews of the time he also had a Greek name, Paul, by which he is best known to Christians and to history. Paul was a member of the Pharisaic sect of Judaism. By his own admission he strove to live in strict adherence to the Law of Moses. Initially Saul persecuted followers of the Way, even demanding the death sentence for them because of their heresy. On the road to Damascus to arrest some of these men and women, he met the risen Jesus who asked Saul why he was persecuting Christ. From that day, Paul became a Christian and an apostle of Jesus. He was not easily accepted in the Christian communities, who knew of his persecution of them. He also struggled to be in unity with the other apostles, with churches to which he came as a preacher, and even with members of churches he helped to found. Paul's letters or epistles mention the persecution suffered by Jewish Christians, affirm the Church's practice of baptism and Eucharist, outline the structures of the new church, teach about the charisms given by the Spirit, declare that all, whether men or women are equally sharers in the divine Sonship of Jesus and in the Spirit, and Paul recounts the great struggle within local Christian communities over the acceptance of non-Jews into this new Church of Christ.

Tensions similar to those Paul experienced mark the Catholic Church to this day and usually get the majority of the media coverage, along with whatever scandals may be available. The news coverage of ongoing struggles include questions of the Church's relationships with Judaism and other religions, relationships with other Christian churches, strife over inclusion of women, and tension between structural and charismatic dimensions of the church. What is less well documented in the media is the continuity of the Church's faith and practice from its infancy in apostolic times to its present hierarchically ordered but uniquely charismatic life. This continuity is the third meaning of Catholic. The Church is Catholic because everything revealed by God in Christ which is necessary for the salvation of the world has been faithfully handed on and is available within the Catholic Church today. The guarantor for this continuity of the means to universal salvation is the Holy Spirit. Because the Church is in the world, it cannot avoid tensions and struggles, but because the Spirit of God is at work in a unique way in the Church, the Catholic Church maintains continuity of faith and practice with the original Apostles and disciples of Jesus. This continuity of faith and practice in the Catholic Church is expressed within the tensions and struggles of its historical experience, particularly as the Church resolves these through the ongoing Spirit inspired development of its teaching and practices. Yet one of the current areas of both tension and doctrinal development concerns the very question, "How is the Catholic Church uniquely different than other churches and Christian communities in maintaining continuity in a unique and universal way with Christ and his Apostles?"

Chapter two offers a history of the early formation of the Catholic Church. The first five centuries of Christian history saw the development of several doctrinal, liturgical, and hierarchical structures that define the Catholic Church, its faith and practices. These characteristics were not formulated for the most part in Europe but in the Middle East, Africa, and present day Italy, Greece, and Turkey. They developed among a rich diversity of peoples and cultures and amidst the great turmoil of the Roman Empire's constant social and political struggles. These civil and political matrixes influenced the development of the Catholic Church in the first five centuries. Over the next five centuries they led to its fracture into a Church of the East and a Church of the West which maintained continuity of faith but not of practical unity. To this day the Church of the West is called the Roman Catholic Church which maintains unity with some Churches of the East. The Oriental and Byzantine Churches of the East, who are not in communion with Rome, called themselves Orthodox. Ultimately, Church authority was the issue around which division occurred, especially the authority of the Bishop of Rome.

The third chapter examines the structures of authority within the Catholic Church. Papal authority is probably the most distinct structure in the Catholic communion. It is of three kinds: bishop, patriarch, and head of the universal church. The Pope, English for *Papa*, is the Bishop of Rome and as such, the head of the local Church at Rome, the diocese that includes the city of Rome. He has traditionally been called the Patriarch of the Western or Roman Church. Historically, some local bishops exercised authority over the appointment of bishops in their region. In this patriarchal system, oversight by a bishop of a particularly important local church linked bishops within geographical areas or cultural groups. This patriarchal system continues to be an important component of Catholic Church unity, especially in the East. The Bishop of Rome has third distinct ministry, a ministry of unity within the Catholic Church as a whole. The Pope holds together in unity the College of Bishops, all the Catholic bishops throughout the world and as such is the visible head of the universal Church. Those local Churches whose Patriarchs and bishops are in communion with the Pope are considered to be Catholic. As center for unity for the College of Bishops, he shares the teaching authority or *Magisterium* in the Church with them. This is the authority to discern and teach the authentic faith handed down by the Apostles. One very controversial and yet firmly held dimension of this ministry of teaching was only gradually defined over the centuries. It is the infallibility of this ministry when it is used in teaching the revealed faith. The infallible teaching authority of the Pope was not declared a doctrine of the faith until 1870 and has been officially invoked only once since.

Authority in the Catholic Church has its conflicts, as does authority in every human affair. One conflict is between the sacramental authority of ordained ministry and the bureaucratic authority of those appointed to administer the bishop's or Pope's authority. Another is between these structures of authority and the personal consciences of the members of the Church who are neither ordained nor hold offices. They, nonetheless, must make decisions according to their own relationship to Jesus, the source of the Church's life and unity expressed through the ordained ministries and their assistant structures. No consideration of authority in the Catholic Church would be complete without some mention of the consensus of faith that must be formed by these various appeals to authority. This discussion leads to chapter four, the Reformation.

The issue of authority was central to the Protestant Reform of the Catholic Church. The place of personal conscience and of the authority of the Scriptures, the scandalous behavior of ordained and bureaucratic ministers, and the economic and cultural tensions that were spawning political development of nations in Europe were all factors in the movement toward reform. Yet, the foundation of the Reformation is not reducible to these issues but is the reason for their importance. The ultimate reason for ongoing reformation, in the life of its members and in all the processes and ministries identified as the Church, is access to and expression of the life of God revealed in Jesus Christ and shared by the Spirit among its members. This was the reason for the protest among Catholics at the time of the Reformation and the stimulus for the Catholic Counter-Reform codified by the Council of Trent. Sharing the free gift of divine life remains the motivating force for all Church reform and was the topic that most occupied the next great Catholic reform introduced in the 1960s by the Second Vatican Council.

Chapter five outlines the influence of the Second Vatican Council on the Catholic Church as it entered its third millennium. Catholic bishops from around the world meeting in Rome declared that God's fundamental intention is to share the holiness of the divine life with each member and through the Church with all humankind. This share in the divine life by all the members is called *communio* or communion of life. The structures of the Church are divinely inspired to accomplish this communion, and the mission of the Church is to engage all human endeavors in it. Consequently, the documents of Vatican II preserved the continuity of the Church's faith and practice and at the same time changed its defensive attitude, operative since Trent, to one of confident engagement with the religions and cultures of the world.

Vatican II and its decrees reflect the vast research into the Church's doctrine and practices that occupied scholars in the nineteenth and early twentieth century. Protestant and Orthodox scholars cooperated in these studies. This ecumenical cooperation led to changes in the relationship among Christian Churches. The United States of America also contributed to the Council through its political experiment in democracy. The Council's declaration on religious freedom resulted from the work of the American theologian John Courtney Murray. He advocated the human right, guaranteed by God, to choose a religious belief even when the choice was not for membership in the Catholic Church. The declaration of the freedom of religious conscience was a clear example of the Church learning from a culture. This declaration changed the Catholic approach to other world religions. Implementation of the Council's other decrees changed the way Catholic ministries, religious education, faith formation, missionary activity, social advocacy, and liturgical worship were conducted.

Despite all of the changes brought about by Vatican II and possibly because of them, one must ask, "What makes the Catholic Church unique among other Christian denominations?" Chapter six offers a response. First, the Catholic Church, while it claims to have a unique status among other Christian bodies, intends that status as a means of unity rather than a mark of difference. Second, the things that are popularly identified as unique to Catholics are often adaptations of ancient practices that are shared by the Orthodox Churches. These practices frequently have roots in other more ancient world religions. Third, the Catholic Church has an admittedly unique relationship to Judaism and has relied on its heritage to develop aspects of its own worship, prayer, and moral teaching. Finally, the Catholic Church's ability to hold together in unity such a marvelous diversity of teachings, cultures, and tensions in its long history, current membership, and ongoing life makes it most unique among other Christian Churches.

Another unique characteristic of the Catholic Church is its prayer life. The prayer of the Church is studied in chapter seven. Catholic prayer is both public or liturgical and private or devotional. All Catholic prayer is primarily based in the Scriptures. These holy writings were either written by the Jews and used by the Church or written by the Church itself. In either case the faith of the Church is that they were written under the influence of the Holy Spirit, who guided the Church in their acceptance and guides it still in their interpretation. The Church's liturgical forms are ritual enactments of the Word of God that make available to the People of God the realities they hear proclaimed. All private prayer is based in *Lectio Divina,* reading the divine revelation, the Bible. The diverse forms of Catholic private prayer make these Scriptures come alive. Private prayer draws on the Church's liturgical prayer, the natural world, and the inner world of human experience. The rich traditions of Catholic private prayer have been developed by men and women who are saints, religious, hermits, pilgrims, and scholars, and are practiced by people of every professional, cultural, and economic group. It is a tradition far too rich to be adequately presented in a small chapter in a single book, but one no book on the Catholic Church can ignore.

Catholic belief in the Communion of Saints, enshrined in its principal creeds, is integral to prayer. The final chapter explains the veneration of the saints and the special honor given to Mary as the Mother of God. Mary is honored by Moslems in great part because of the Catholic honor given to Mary as the Mother of Jesus, whom Islam acknowledges as a prophet. Catholic devotion to Mary and the saints is often confused with a distancing of the devotee from God. This is something that the Church is vigilant to correct. The actual intent of prayer and other honors directed to Mary and the saints is to experience ever more deeply the communion of the devotee with the Father and the Son and the Holy Spirit, whose divine life is revealed in the Maternity of Mary and the lives of the saints. It is this communion which is the essence of the Church.

It is the hope of the author that those who read this book will come to appreciate the desire of the Catholic Church to bring into communion all the disparate tensions of human life and to draw them into the kingdom of God.

2
The Continuity of Faith

The Catholic Church formally began when the first disciples of Jesus received the Spirit of God at Pentecost, fifty days after the Passover. His disciples spread the Gospel of Jesus Christ throughout the Jewish communities that populated the Roman Empire. These local communities admitted non-Jews and grew into assemblies of Christians. Today, the Catholic Church is the union of these local assemblies or churches which share communion with each other. Communion is a way of life rooted in a continuity of faith as preached by the Apostles and lived out in communities under the care of their successors. The content of the apostolic preaching and communion of life is called the Catholic Tradition and is found fully in the Catholic Church. The Catholic Church is divided into Churches which follow different Rites. The Rites follow the customs and practices either of the Roman Church and are known as Roman Catholics or of the Churches of the East known as Byzantine or Oriental Catholics. Byzantine Catholics follow the customs of Constantinople and Oriental Catholics the customs of various other ancient local Churches. All of these Churches with their Rites are united in one Catholic Church by the faith that comes from the Apostles.

The Catholic Tradition is found at least partially in other Churches and Christian communities that do not share in full communion with the Catholic Church. The Catholic Church holds that the Orthodox Churches are in continuity with the apostolic faith but not in communion with the Pope. Thus the Orthodox Churches lack the full expression of the Catholic faith. Protestant Churches are Christian communities which lack both communion with the Catholic Church and the fullness of the apostolic faith. The relationship between communion of life and continuity of faith is integral to the Catholic or Universal Church. If communion of life fails, can there be continuity with the apostolic faith? Any division among churches calls into question their continuity with the apostolic faith. This chapter examines the continuity of faith and the communion of life that has marked the Catholic Church since the first outpouring of the Spirit.

A Trinitarian Faith

Catholicism is a revealed religion. Catholics believe God personally revealed something no one could otherwise discover or know. What God revealed is that God is unity in *communio*, communion. Through God's self-revelation, Catholics believe humankind now is included in the divine communion, the life of the Trinity.

Specifically, Catholics believe that the measure of creation, the Word by which God made all things, was incarnated in the man Jesus of Nazareth. Jesus called himself the Son of Man. By using that title Jesus showed he shared everything it means to be human. However, Son of Man in the Jewish Scriptures also designated someone God exalted above all human powers. His disciples called Jesus the Son of God and claimed God had revealed this relationship. The evidence that Jesus is the Son of God from all eternity is that God raised him from the dead after he was crucified, died, and was buried for three days. As he promised before his death, the risen Jesus sent the Spirit upon his disciples. This Spirit drew the disciples of Jesus into the same relationship he himself had with God and so confirmed the teaching of Jesus that they also should call God their Father.

Catholics believe that they share what all humankind is called to share, the life of God. Catholicism teaches that there is one God who is a Trinity. The Trinity is a divine unity of life shared in a hierarchical communion. This communion of life is shared by the Father who sends his Word into the world and pours out the Holy Spirit. The Spirit comes from the Father upon those who accept both Jesus as God's

Son and his coming among us as the evidence of God's love for the world. Catholics believe that the members of the Church share now in this divine communion, wherein they have the forgiveness of sins and the promise of resurrection and eternal life. Catholics believe all creation is invited into this same communion of life with the Trinity.

Catholics believe their way of life together is a share in the life of God, as that life has been revealed through Jesus Christ by the power of the Holy Spirit. The Catholic Tradition is the continuity of this faith from the original Apostles and disciples of Jesus as it continues to be lived in the Church. This apostolic faith is expressed through the Church's liturgy and sacraments, in its adherence to the revealed Word of God, and by a communion of life among the members that is held in unity by hierarchical leadership. These three dimensions of the Catholic Tradition are empowered and directed by the Spirit of God. Together they are the source both of the unity of life and practice shared among its members, and of the Church's doctrinal and moral teachings which flow from that life.

Continuity with God's Revelation to Israel

Those who believed Jesus of Nazareth was the Christ were known after his resurrection as followers of the Way. Most of them were Jews who spread the news of his resurrection through the Jewish synagogues. Synagogues existed in communities throughout the

Roman Empire and beyond, and were gathering places for Jews and for Gentiles interested in Judaism. Some of these Jews and their Jewish sympathizers believed that Jesus was the Messiah foretold by Moses and the prophets. *Messiah* is Hebrew and means the anointed one who is sent by God. It is translated into Greek as *Christos*. In conformity with Jewish practice, the believers expressed their unity by accepting followers of the Way from other Jewish communities and by extending hospitality to them and their ministries. The followers of the Way soon became known as Christians but by the year 80 were no longer accepted in the synagogues. Their way of life as followers of Jesus, the Christ, could no longer be maintained in unity with Judaism. That brought into question the continuity of their faith with Judaism, the faith of Abraham and Moses.

At issue in their dismissal from the synagogues was their continuity with the faith of Abraham and the Law of God given through Moses. Christian apostles and teachers labored to show that in fact Jesus was the fulfillment of all that had been foretold in the Jewish Scriptures, known subsequently among them as the Old Testament. Christians continued to use these Jewish texts. They added various letters from the Apostles and other Christian writers to these sacred writings, most notably the four Gospels, four unique accounts of the life, ministry, death, and resurrection of Jesus. Some of the Christian Scriptures were written within twenty years of the death of Jesus. The last books were written by the end of the first century or sixty years after the proclamation of Christ's resurrection. These texts formed a New Testament, one purpose of which was to show that their faith in Jesus as the Christ and Son of God was in continuity with the faith of Abraham and Moses. In fact, they labored under the guidance of the Spirit to show that the Jewish religion found its fulfillment in the Way which Christ had opened to a share in God's life.

The Jewish and Christian Scriptures, the Old and New Testaments, were read together as the Word of God in assemblies of Christians during rites such as baptism or Sunday gatherings for the Lord's Supper. The Scriptures and the rites were inseparable. The prophets had announced the work of God in Christ ages before the full revelation was made through his earthly life and ministry. The New Testament showed that the prophetic utterances were fulfilled in Christ. Ritual actions, as attested in the Christian Scriptures, celebrated the Church's mysterious share in the life of God given through the death and resurrection of Jesus Christ and by the power of Spirit. At the same time, these rites together with the Christian Scriptures affirmed the continuity of the Church's faith with the faith of the prophets. Together they affirmed the communion of the Church's life with the life of holiness to which God called Israel through the faith of Abraham and the teachings of Moses. On the other hand, these rites and the New Testament writings increasingly came to express the Church's separation from Judaism's community of life.

The continued growth of Christian communities was organized under local Christian overseers, called in Greek either *episcopoi* or *presbyteroi*, that is bishops or presbyters/elders. Their ministry was confirmed within their communities by the Spirit as continuous with the authority of the Apostles. Their task was twofold. They were to confirm the continuity of the community's faith and hold together the corporate unity of the believers. Gradually, some bishops began to exercise greater influence and even authority over bishops within their cultural and political spheres. These were known as Patriarchs. Over the centuries, the authority of the Bishop of Rome was recognized as a specialized ministry holding the Patriarchs and bishops and their local Churches in unity of life and continuity of faith. What today is known as the Catholic Church is the union of these bishops and their Churches throughout the world with the Church of Rome and its Bishop, the Pope.

Ultimately what is means to be Catholic is not reducible simply to this hierarchical ministry. The reason the Church calls itself Catholic is the continuity of its faith with the self-revelation of God and its unity as the Communion of Saints in the life of the Trinity. It is this unity and continuity which the hierarchical ministries are meant to serve. For Catholics it is *communio* that binds together the multitudes around the world and across the millennia to the faith of Abraham and Moses as it is fulfilled in Christ.

Catholic Christianity

After two thousand years of growth and with all the changes that necessarily have accumulated, is it reasonable to believe that the Catholic Church is in any way the same reality as the original community of people who knew Jesus of Nazareth during his earthly ministry, witnessed his death and resurrection, and received the first outpouring of the Spirit? What is at stake is whether the Catholic Church is the true growth of the seed planted by Jesus or some strange growth that he would not recognize. More profoundly, is the Catholic Church able to offer persons a share in Christ's own life with God who anointed him with the Spirit and sent him into the world?

Questions about the continuity of the Church's faith with the teaching and life of Christ began with the teaching of the Apostles. The first of many such debates was the inclusion of non-Jews as followers of Christ. Was this the intent of Christ, who seemed to be sent to Israel and not to the Gentiles? The Acts of the Apostles indicated that first Peter and then Paul were sent by God to settle this issue of unity and continuity. Traditionalist Jewish members strongly objected to this innovation. Peter testified the Spirit directed his acceptance of the Gentiles. Paul defended himself and his practice of inclusion by claiming the direction of the same Spirit. The Jerusalem community, under the leadership of the Apostle James and inspired by the Spirit, found confirmation in the Old Testament that it was God's plan to join Gentiles with Jews through faith in Christ. Finally there was a general, although gradual, acceptance of Gentiles into the practice of the faith in local communities at Rome and throughout the Empire. Guided by the Spirit, these Churches recognized that inclusion strengthened the faith of the whole assembly in the gratuitous nature of God's salvation in Christ. This was the first experience of what it meant to be Catholic, the inclusion of all those who believed, Jew and Gentile, in one communion of life with God.

The resolution of the Gentile issue indicated how the Catholic Churches would continue to resolve questions of faith and life. Specifically, the teaching of the Apostles gave validity to the Church's continuity with Jesus. They had been with Jesus in his earthly ministry and could witness that he had been crucified, that he died, and was buried. The Apostles saw and talked with him after his resurrection. They had received a share in the power of his resurrection, the Spirit of God who was the guarantor of the truth they taught concerning Jesus. Next, Christians found texts in the writings of the Jewish law, prophets, and psalms inspired by the Spirit that validated the inclusion of Gentiles in their communities of faith. Finally, there was a general, although gradual, acceptance of Gentiles into the practice of the faith based on the experience of local communities.

Guided by the Spirit they recognized that such inclusion strengthened the faith of the whole assembly.

These touchstones remain to this day the guiding principles for unity and continuity of faith and life among Catholic Christians. They are interdependent dimensions of the living Catholic Tradition. First among them is the work of the Spirit. Without the working of the Spirit of God nothing can be in communion. Next is the testimony of the Apostles, recorded in the words of the New Testament and experienced in the sacraments of the Church which hand on the apostolic faith in ritual action. The witness given by their apostolic leadership continues in the Church through their successors, the bishops. At times this apostolic leadership has been interpreted as the physical ordination of individual bishops in an unbroken line from the first twelve Apostles. That is, however, too physically absolute to be historically accurate. Apostolic leadership is more correctly understood as a relationship of communion within the leadership of the Church. Bishops through their election and ordination are inserted by the Spirit into the College of Bishops which as a body is the successor of the Apostles. The work of the Spirit also enlivens and guides the other principles of continuity. The validity of scriptural evidence is dependent upon the Spirit who inspired the writing of the Scriptures, and confirmed their inspiration through their acceptance by the Church. The apostolic leadership, the College of Bishops, authentically teaches the content of the Scriptures in the Church under the guidance of the Spirit. The Spirit works in the faithful as they accept these teachings as integral with their community of life in the Church. The final evidence of the continuity of the Church's faith is the acceptance by the members of the Church of the resolution of a question of faith or practice, however gradually achieved. On the other hand, continuity is also maintained by the faithful asking their leadership for clarification of Catholic life and practice. While the unity of believers is maintained through these principles of communion, it is important to note that these principles do not guarantee immediate results or easy resolution of controversies.

The Church, while it offers a share in the divine life, lives in the complex social and political circumstances of this world. These circumstances raise questions that may take centuries to solve. By 80 C.E. (the Common Era for Jews and Christians), Christians, both Jew and Gentile, were thrown out as heretics from the very synagogues which for four decades had been their incubators. This schism raised a serious question. Were the Jews, who did not accept Christ, responsible for his death and consequently condemned by God? Were their descendants who rejected and persecuted his followers also in some way responsible for his death? The Scriptural evidence appeared contradictory. The Letter to the Hebrews and several Gospel passages appeared to condemn those Jews who did not receive the Christ.

Paul wrote in his letter to the Romans that Jewish non-acceptance of Christ was part of God's plan. While their rejection of him benefited Christians, Paul could not say how the Jews would finally share in Christ's redemption of the world, only that God's promises to them were permanent. This issue remained a serious controversy into the twentieth century and contributed to the social and political environment that spawned the Holocaust.

From the time of the Apostles, the Catholic Church recognized that it sprang from the religion of Israel and is in continuity with the precepts and promises given by God to the Jewish People through their patriarchs and prophets. The Church, from the time of the Apostle Paul, also believed and declared that all these laws and promises are fulfilled through Jesus of Nazareth for those who profess faith in him within the Catholic Church. In various ages Catholic theologians sought the cooperation of Jewish rabbis in the study of the ancient Jewish texts in order to better understand their own Christian faith. The Catholic Church finally and clearly declared in the twentieth century that the promises of God to the Jewish people remain and that salvation may be attained by them through faithfulness to their patriarchal religion. While much progress has been accomplished in the relations between these two Abrahamic religions, the potential for controversy continues in the actual relationships between Catholic and

Jews, especially since the development in the last century of the secular State of Israel.

It took the Catholic Church two millennia to resolve the theological question of the relationship between Jews and Christians. Christian communities themselves were repeatedly divided over other issues of faith that arose as early as the first century. Some of the earliest disagreements were over whether Jesus was really raised from the dead, whether he was Son of God and equal to the Father, and whether he was able to give his body for food and blood as true drink to his followers. These disagreements are attested in the New Testament, particularly in the letters of Paul and the writings of the Apostle John. Other controversies were added over the centuries. Even the manner of solving these controversies was the source of still more divisions among Christians. One way to understand the Catholic Church is to study these divisions. However, another is to examine a few of the creative ways the Church preserved its communion and the continuity of its Catholic faith in the face of various threats.

The First Centuries

The initial spread of the Gospel of Jesus Christ has been associated with the Roman Empire. Jesus was put to death by Roman crucifixion, and the New Testament was originally written by persons in congregations within the Roman Empire. What is not as well understood is that the Gospel was addressed to people of diverse cultures within that Empire and spread rapidly beyond its borders. The proclamation of the Gospel was shaped and developed by the diverse peoples who received it. Their cultures and languages shaped and developed the way in which local Christian communities understood and practiced their faith in Christ. These understandings and practices were as diverse as the peoples and cultures that had received the Good News. How then was the continuity of faith and the unity of life and practice tested and maintained?

The New Testament made it clear that the Church is a living community to be entered and not simply a message to be understood. It was in just such communities of faith and practice that the New Testament was written. Certain practices accompanied the Gospel proclamation wherever it traveled. The Good News about Jesus spread together with rituals which shared his life and authority within communities of his disciples. Those who went out from Jerusalem in the first century baptized or encouraged their hearers to be baptized. Along with baptism which all members must undergo, all the members were invited to share the Eucharist, the Lord's Supper. Baptism and the sharing of the Lord's Supper were practiced in Christian communities where the New Testament was being written, and where the Apostles were handing on their authority to other leaders in the Church. A third ritual, the laying on of hands, was used to designate apostolic leadership within communities of faith. Some of these leaders in turn laid hands on successors imparting to them a share in the Spirit who empowered and guided the Apostles. Both Paul and John, in the face of opposition, taught through their writings in the New Testament the true meaning of these practices for the followers of Jesus. The Catholic Church is a living community which has maintained these same scriptures and practices and hands them on to succeeding generations within diverse cultures.

The four Gospels testify to the diversity of cultures and viewpoints extant in the early Church. They are not simply a record of what had happened to Jesus. The Gospels are interpretations, the way in which diverse communities understood his life, ministry, death and resurrection. Other New Testament writings also interpret the meaning of God's revelation in Christ. Individual books focus the interpretation through the lifestyle in a given place where a Gospel was written or to which an Apostle addressed a letter. The community of life and practice that bound Christians together in Christ confirmed the continuity of their faith with the apostolic preaching. One could not be shared aside from the other. Faith and communion of life interpenetrated each other in the living organism of the Church. So complete was this rooting of continuity of faith in the life and practices of the local churches that the scriptures were tested over time to see if they reflected the community's faith and practice. In this way, discrete pieces of scripture gained acceptance as inspired by the

Spirit and were enrolled in the canon of the Old or New Testament.

The gradual canonization of the New Testament, or establishment of a rule by which to determine its inspired content, occurred over a period of at least three centuries. The Old Testament books currently listed in a Catholic Bible were accepted as early as 170 C.E. in the western part of the Roman Empire. Final agreement in the eastern part of the empire was not settled until 692. Justin, a philosopher and martyr at Rome, wrote in 163 C.E. that the Gospels and apostolic letters were read on Sundays at the celebration of the Lord's Supper. Still it was not until 367 C.E. that Anthanasius, the Patriarch of Alexandria in Egypt, published the definitive canon of the New Testament which was also agreed to by a local council held at Rome in 382.

This long period of testing may seem odd to the contemporary reader who has doubtless heard that the Bible is the book that sets Christians apart. The point is the Bible was written under the inspiration of the Spirit within the Church at the same time the ordained ministries and the sacramental rites were being practiced. The Bible was written by the Church under the inspiration of the Spirit. The local Churches under the influence of the same Spirit accepted these books as revealed by God because the writings expressed their faith and practice. The Catholic Church believes only Churches in continuity with that faith and practice are able to authentically interpret the Bible. Their official teachers are the Bishops of these communities.

Catholic Life and Practices

The moral teaching of the Church has been an expression of Catholic life from its beginning. Teaching morals is a way of authentically interpreting the Word of God. Jesus challenged the legalism of the Pharisee party of the Jews and insisted instead on mercy. He taught a strict code against divorce and set out specific practices for fraternal correction and forgiveness of sins. Christ insisted those who harm children and the marginalized will receive the most severe punishment from God. Paul required sexual morality among Christians and practices of charitable sharing of resources. The Apostle James commanded control over the tongue and the care of widows and orphans. Anyone aware of the Jewish Scripture will notice its continuity with the ethical concerns of these teachers. Catholic opposition to abortion and infanticide was expressed in writing as early as the middle of the second century. The care of pilgrims, travelers, the sick, widows, orphans, and the poor are attested to in the Christian Scriptures. These practices attracted new converts throughout the first three centuries even in the face of Roman persecution. It was usual among pagan Romans to express piety by caring for members of one's family, political party, or religious group. What made Christians so unusual was the way they loved and cared for the stranger as if for a god. Indeed, the hallmark of Christian charity was to receive each person as if he or she were Christ. Therein is the foundation for all Catholic moral teaching. Each human person has unique and unrepeatable dignity and value because he or she shares in his or her own humanity the image of the Beloved Son of God.

Monasticism was another dimension of Catholic life developed in the first centuries. Catholic Christians developed, as early as the First Letter of Paul to the Corinthians, a reverence for life-long virginity and withdrawal from the world. Romans had their Vestal Virgins and the pagan Cybele religion had its castrated priesthood, but these were not the roots of Christian virginity and monasticism. The roots of these Christian practices arose in the Gospel preaching of Jesus. He spoke of those who forsook marriage for the sake of the Kingdom and of those who gave up all earthly possessions, even their lives, for its sake. Paul taught the time was short for Jesus to return and that it was best to live without a spouse so as to dedicate oneself to the Lord. However, the influence of Catholicism's pagan political and cultural context did influence its early reverence for these practices. For instance, the persecutions and martyrdom of Christians in the first centuries inspired some to live the white martyrdom of voluntary celibate chastity. Mideastern peoples had traditions of holy hermits and reverenced those ascetics who lived without earthly pleasures. Some pagan philosophers and religious cults shunned the material world because it was the place where the pure spirit was trapped in flesh or in which the evil movements of the flesh overwhelmed the mind and spirit. All of these influenced the Catholic attitude toward virginity and various monastic practices but were not their spiritual seedbed.

The spiritual seedbed of the Catholic practices of celibate chastity and monasticism is the desire to live the life of the Trinity here on earth. Since Jesus is the Incarnation of God, all flesh has the capacity to reveal God. All creation is sacramental. The human person is particularly the sacrament by which God has revealed the mystery of divine life, hidden from all eternity but now made flesh in Christ. Monasticism is a personal search for the life revealed by Christ as it is lived out in Christian community.

Some of the first hermits and monastics were Christians whose family or community members were martyred. They withdrew from the world and lived as if they were dead to all but God. Those who followed them wanted simply to live their lives on earth in union with God and neighbor as if already in heaven. Hermits lived in solitude, monastics in community. Both observed celibate chastity as a way to follow the example of Jesus, whom tradition knew as celibate himself. Jewish tradition allowed a man to set aside spouse and worldly affairs for a time so as to be transformed by the glory of the Lord through the prayerful study of the

Scriptures. Jesus taught that there were those who could accept such a gift from God.

From the first century, Christians sought to live the charism of celibacy. By the second century there were men and women who vowed themselves to lifelong celibacy and gave themselves over to contemplation of the Scriptures. They sought a share in the divine transformation as their daily way of life on earth, to live in the image of the Beloved Son of God who gave up all things to establish the Kingdom of his Father.

These practices are examples of the Catholic Church's desire to seek continuity in all things with the self-revelation of God in Christ by the power of the Holy Spirit. Catholics believe God's self-revelation empowers their Church's worship and teachings, life and practices, and offers communion with God to the whole human community, indeed to every creature.

3
Authority in the Church

The lines of authority in the Catholic Church are fascinatingly complex. Centuries of growth and development overlay its structures and practices. Part one of this chapter will illustrate this complexity by reviewing such material as the election of popes and the persecution of Christians. In the Church, ordained leadership and its bureaucracy can cause confusion. Part two will examine tensions between interpenetrating systems of authority. These are sacramental versus bureaucratic authority, and charismatic gifts versus hierarchical structures. All become members of Christ's Body through sacramental baptism; bishops by sacramental ordination share in Christ's headship over the Body. A bishop's share in Christ's headship is both a charism and a hierarchical structure. It is a gift, a charism, given to the bishop personally by the Spirit, but at the same time this charism hierarchically structures the Church so that all the members may receive

Christ's shepherding through the ministry of the bishop. Bishops in turn set up agencies composed of laity, religious, and ordained persons to assist them in the exercise of their headship. Ordained and bureaucratic leadership tend to intermingle and become somewhat confusing in their forms. Bureaucratic agencies function as pastoral expressions of the pope or bishop's leadership, but also have great influence on their leadership. These agencies bridge the hierarchical ministry of succeeding popes and bishops. They influence the implementation of the pope's or bishop's policies during their tenure. They also form their successors, who are usually members of the bureaucracy and limit the potential for these successors to change policies and practices in the Church.

There is a necessary tension between charism and hierarchy, sacramental ordination and bureaucracy. Charism and hierarchy are both the work of the Spirit of God in the Church. They are not supposed to be in competition but in tension. The Spirit uses tension between these diverse elements to create unity. Yet the question remains: is bureaucracy given by the Spirit as a charism or a hierarchical structure? Or does bureaucracy betray the fact that it is not Spirit inspired by instigating competition in the Church, as sociology indicates it does in every human endeavor?

Part I - Authority's Historical Complexity

The Election of Popes and Bishops

The election of popes and bishops has changed dramatically over the centuries. Catholic Christians in first and second century Rome elected their bishop, following a practice akin to the ancient Roman Senate's election of chiefs of state. The presbyters, who today are called priests, elected one of their members to serve as the *episcopos*, meaning overseer. He was a married man with a family, and early in the Church's history may even have served a term as Bishop of Rome and then returned to the ranks of the presbyteral senate which would elect a new *episcopos*. Lifetime service in the episcopal ministry became the norm during the first four centuries, unless a man resigned or was deposed because of some moral, doctrinal, or political reason. Lifetime service in the office of bishop was terminated when exile intervened or often ended in martyrdom.

In the early centuries, bishops were elected by the clergy with varying degrees of participation by the Catholic populace. Upon their election, bishops in the west sent letters to the Bishop of Rome asking to be extended communion with him. In the east, a bishop would request communion with his local Metropolitan or Patriarch, who were bishops of major cities in a region. One factor considered in extending communion was whether the person had been validly elected, but every bit as important was whether he maintained the same faith as the other bishops, the faith handed on by the Apostles. While bishops would appeal to the Pope for communion with him, once he was validly elected, the Bishop of Rome would not appeal for communion but received from them declarations of communion with him. To this day, after electing the Pope, the Cardinals' first act, after certifying the validity of the election, is to offer their declaration of communion with him. The ancient custom of the Roman clergy electing the Pope is recalled each time a pope appoints someone as a Cardinal. On such occasions, a pope gives a Cardinal the ceremonial pastoral care of one of the many churches in the city of Rome or its vicinity.

One famous case of the clergy and the populace electing the bishop of a city is Ambrose's election at Milan in 374. He was elected before he was even baptized. His election reflects the social and religious conditions at that time. Ambrose was the Roman governor of Milan, the major Imperial administrative city in Italy in the late 300s. Rome and much of western Empire had deteriorated under barbarian invasions. In fact the Empire was rife with political and civil unrest for three centuries before it finally collapsed in 476. After 313, when Catholic Christianity was recognized as a legal religious practice within the Empire, bishops grew in civil importance. At Rome and in many other cities, the bishop was responsible for the civil as well as the spiritual welfare of the members of the Church. Meanwhile, divisions among Christians over differences in practice and doctrine created deep unrest. Someone with Ambrose's administrative skills was needed in the midst of this turmoil. After his election as bishop, Ambrose was baptized and ordained. He served with distinction and remains to this day an exemplar of episcopal leadership.

State interference in the election of a bishop, patriarch, or pope was a common phenomenon in Catholic history. As recently as 1903, the Austro-Hungarian Empire maintained a veto in the election of any one Cardinal to the Papacy. Constantine, the first Christian Emperor, declared himself the equal of the Apostles and began appointing bishops or at least confirming their election. Eventually that right was sought by kings and emperors in Christian and non-Christian states. Some Catholic monarchs used their authority to appoint bishops to reform corruption in the Church. Over the centuries, other political leaders strove through the appointment of bishops to control Church affairs or co-opt the Church for purposes of State. In response, the Popes worked to bring the election of bishops under their own authority. In 1911, Pius X finally was able to secure the independent election by popes of all bishops in France.

Popes attained unusual freedom in the appointment of bishops in the United States of America. In 1788, Rome wanted to appoint John Carroll as

America's first Catholic bishop and vetted his name with the Federal Government to see if there would be any objection. The official response was that such appointments could not be reviewed by the government because of the non-establishment of religion clause in the recently ratified American Constitution. Meanwhile, Carroll insisted upon being elected by the clergy rather than being appointed without their consent. He obtained all but two of the priests' votes in the original thirteen states. In 1789, the Pope appointed John Carroll as the first Bishop of Baltimore. Rome never again allowed the clergy in the U.S. to vote in the election of a bishop. To this day, however, Rome wants to make sure that the appointment of a bishop will not bring about civil condemnation or scandal.

Rome and the Communist government of China are currently negotiating over such issues. After the Communist takeover of China, the government rejected all foreign control over religious activities in China and has continued to appoint all the Catholic bishops. For at least the last two decades, Rome has privately approved the majority of these ordinations beforehand or subsequently legitimatized them. Recently, Papal approval has been publicly declared at the ordination of government-appointed bishops, and the government in China seems to have politely turned a deaf ear.

Languages, Cultures, and Governance

Differences in culture and language between Romans and Orientals made it difficult for Christians to maintain their unity. During the first four centuries, the Catholic Church spread east beyond the Roman Empire into the Persian Empire, present day Iran, and into kingdoms in Mesopotamia, now Iraq. As always, it was difficult for persons who spoke diverse languages to enter into each other's worlds and see things from the perspective of the alien culture. Different languages made differing doctrinal formulations necessary to preserve the same faith. The differing doctrinal expressions caused separation among Catholic Churches. The Oriental Churches separated from the Catholic Churches inhabiting the Roman Empire. Even within that Empire, Catholic liturgies and doctrinal formulations varied markedly between the Roman west and Byzantine east. Centuries earlier Roman legions had taken over Greek kingdoms established by the followers of Alexander the Great after his death, and adopted the Greek language and culture. By the late 300s, Latin replaced Greek as the common language of the Western Roman Empire. Byzantine Catholics, who continued to express their faith in Greek, objected to western Latin doctrinal statements that seemed to radically change the faith. Most notably they objected to the addition in the Nicene Creed of the *filioque*, a term which defined the sending of the Spirit by the Father "and the Son." Eventually, the Byzantine Churches separated from

Rome and called themselves Orthodox Churches. Today, *filioque* is not used at Papal ceremonies when the Creed is recited in Greek, only when Latin is used. Nevertheless, its use remains a point of disagreement between Orthodox and Catholic Churches.

By the fourth century, Roman civil reorganization added pressure on Church unity. Diocletian restructured the Roman Empire in 286 C.E. He divided a single empire, once ruled from Rome, into an eastern and a western region. By 330, Constantine established a new capital at Constantinople for the eastern region, known as Byzantium. Its bishop quickly became the Patriarch around whom the Greek-speaking Churches gathered and became second only to the Pope at Rome in prestige. This created tensions with more ancient Patriarchates, Antioch in Syria and Alexandria in Egypt, who previously exerted influence on the churches in the east. Antioch developed its theology from the point of view of Christ's humanity and Alexandria began from his divinity. Together they created the Church's doctrinal belief in Christ's full humanity and divinity. These Patriarchal Churches claimed foundation by one of the original Apostles or Evangelists. Alexandria claimed the Evangelist Mark. Antioch recalled that Peter taught in its Church, but also knew that Thomas ministered among them. In the early centuries missionaries from Antioch's Patriarchate went as far as Southern India and founded churches there in the line of the Apostle Thomas. Other Patriarchal Churches also claimed descent from one of the original Apostles of Jesus. Jerusalem claimed the entire college of Apostles as its first leaders. Rome was the only Patriarchal Church in the west. It reverenced Peter and Paul not only as teachers of its faith but also as martyrs who confirmed the faith of the Church of Rome with their own blood. As such, the Roman Church held the most ancient claim to the whole of the Catholic Tradition. While all bishops in the early Church were considered Vicars of Christ the Good Shepherd, the Bishop of Rome had the clearest claim to being also the Vicar of Peter. It was on Peter that Christ bestowed the keys of heaven and the commission to feed his sheep. The Bishop of Rome, consequently, could claim to be the center of unity among all the bishops of the Church. Constantinople, on the other hand, claimed its foundation from Andrew, the brother of Peter and the Apostle without whom Peter would not have been introduced to Christ. All these Patriarchs confirmed the election of bishops within their own regions and the communion of church within the Patriarchal region. Nevertheless, the earliest testimony of Christian writers recognized the Church of Rome and its episcopal ministry as the center for unity among all the Catholic Churches. Papal leadership had the double effect of overcoming political divisions within the Roman Empire and contributing to divisions in the Church.

Initially, a pope's ministry of unity was one of charity, affirming orthodoxy in faith and communion in practice. As a sign of this ministry of unity, Papal legates presided at the first seven Ecumenical Councils. Papal authority, however, was both tested and expanded over the centuries in response to internal and external pressures on the Church. It eventually became a source of schism. The universal authority of the Roman Pope was asserted at least as early as the tenth century but was a point of separation between the Roman and Byzantine Churches by 1054. Since then Roman Catholics comprised the majority in the Catholic Church but have maintained unity with the Eastern Church by creating parallel Patriarchates for the Byzantine and Oriental Churches who have returned to communion with Rome. This means that there are both Catholic and Orthodox Churches in the same locales. These opposing jurisdictions have continued to foster conflicts and difficulty in establishing reunion. Pope John Paul II had a keen interest in reuniting the Church east and west and asked in the 1990s how the ministry of the Bishop of Rome might be reformulated to create unity rather than division in the Church. He recognized Roman doctrinal formulations made communion more difficult. The First Vatican Council declared the doctrine of Infallibility in 1870. Infallibility means that the Pope in union with the College of Bishops is the highest authority in the Church. Under the guidance of the Holy Spirit, the Pope will teach all that is necessary for the continuity of faith and the preservation of communion of life in the

Church. The Orthodox held that an Ecumenical Council was the highest authority in the Church. However, the Council also declared the universal pastoral authority of the Bishop of Rome. Universal pastoral authority allowed the Bishop of Rome to implement his teachings should conflict arise with a local bishop or members of the Church. The Orthodox hold that bishops are equal in their authority over their own churches. Papal universal jurisdiction is a serious stumbling block to unity with the Orthodox Churches.

Kings and Bishops

Constantine legitimized Christianity within the Empire. Although not baptized until just before his death in 337, as Emperor he declared himself the equal of the Apostles in the governance of the Church. Constantine appointed bishops and convened the Council of Nicea in 325 to settle a dispute among the churches over whether Christ was fully God and fully man. Nicea was the first universal gathering of the bishops of the Church since the Apostles had met in Jerusalem to settle the question of Gentile membership. It is known as the first Ecumenical Council, from the Greek for household, meaning it gathered the entire household of God. The role of the Emperor, as an overseer of the bishops and their councils, was yet another factor dividing the Church between east and west. The election of the Bishop of Rome was confirmed by the Emperor in the west and that of the

Patriarch of Constantinople by the Emperor in the east. In turn, it became the custom for pope or patriarch to crown these emperors. These mutually legitimatizing relationships led to allegiances, collusion, and conflict between civil and religious rulers. Civil politics created friction between the pope and the patriarch. Pope Leo III crowned Charlemagne as the Holy Roman Emperor in 800 A.D. This act was the final political split between the west and the Byzantine Emperor in Constantinople backed by the Patriarch of Constantinople. This political rupture in turn birthed the schism between the Roman and Byzantine Churches in the eleventh century.

The Medieval feudal system in the west and the Byzantine court system in the east contributed rights and privileges to the Church's hierarchy. Most bishops were members of the nobility. Bishops ruled the Churches as any nobleman would his fief. A bishop's court like any royal court ruled by decree and judged local issues. Popes stressed their authority as head of the Church on earth, sometimes in imitation of the power of kings and emperors. They did so particularly in opposition to rulers who attempted to control the wealth and influence of the Church. Papal sanctioning of coronations led to the common practice of popes and bishops confirming the legitimacy of monarchs, even anointing them with consecrated oil used in the ordination of bishops. This intermingling of the authority of bishops and monarchs led to corruption. Popes, scholars, and members of the nobility led reforms against the sale of holy offices in the Church, known as simony, and the appointment of relatives and friends to positions of authority and financial remuneration, known as nepotism. Both the civil authorities and the hierarchy of the Church struggled with other forms of corruption, including sexual scandals among the clergy and heresy among the faithful. The hierarchy generally claimed the sole right to discipline the clergy but often engaged the civil authorities in quelling unorthodox practices and doctrines among the laity. Kings and emperors claimed the right to invest bishops with the insignia of their office, the crosier or pastoral staff and the episcopal ring, to the further confusion of lines of authority. Known as lay investiture, this controversial practice was condemned over and over again by popes and eventually by a General Council of the Church. The use of authority in the Church has continued internally to mimic civil authority structures and to suffer the consequences of Church policies being enmeshed with the policies of secular regimes.

Persecutions

At the beginning of the Christian era, Romans worshiped a mixture of Greek and Roman deities. Emperors were worshipped as descendants of some of these gods and goddesses. Traditionally, the Emperor alone could approve the official public practice of religions. The Emperors approved cults in which the principal deity enhanced their personal authority or worship.

Catholic Christians worshipped the one God of the Jews, and Jesus whom he sent as Savior and Lord. Catholic worship thus competed with the Emperor's claim to be the savior of world peace and order, whom the gods approved as lord. Christian worship of the One God meant they were unable to participate in those State sponsored activities — sporting events, theatre, and military service — that incorporated public adoration of the Emperor. These restrictions further marginalized Christians and contributed to their being suspect as subversives within the society.

Persecution was sporadic over the first four centuries. Martyrdom affected the Church in two principal ways. First, it placed emphasis on the hierarchical structure of the Church. Under threat of persecution, strong central leadership was paramount. Ignatius, the Bishop of Antioch, stressed the importance of unity with the bishop in letters he wrote to local churches on his way to martyrdom at Rome in 107. Ignatius described a tripartite clergy already existing at the beginning of the second century. These were bishop, presbyters and deacons. Ignatius repeatedly stressed the importance of the unity of the clergy and the laity with the bishop. The second effect of persecutions was to foster a new way of life in the Church, the way followed by hermits and monastics. Because of the witness of the martyrs, men and women withdrew from the world to dedicate themselves to asceticism and prayer for the sake of the Kingdom of God. They became "athletes of the desert" in imitation of the athleticism of the martyrs in the arenas. Their vocation was considered a charism from the Spirit. This charismatic gift lived on in multiple communities of men and women vowed to poverty, chastity and obedience. These religious communities in their turn developed hierarchical structures to secure their way of life and ministries. Civil persecutions contributed both to charismatic and hierarchical developments.

Persecutions also contributed to divisions around the way lapsed members of the community should be reconciled, and the development of the rite of reconciliation. The Letter to the Hebrews posed a question regarding first century Christians who denied Christ in the face of Jewish persecution and returned to the practice of Judaism. Could they ever rejoin the Church? In the following centuries, similar questions regarding Christians under Roman persecution gave birth to schisms. Could Christians who denied their faith in Christ in order to preserve their lives, families, positions, and property ever be reconciled to the Church? What should be done with clergy who lapsed from the faith? Should they be allowed to minister and, if so, should they be re-ordained? These controversies were as intensely debated as current issues concerning clergy who have broken their vows of celibacy, especially any who abused children. The Church's sacrament of penance or rite of reconciliation was particularly important in responding to these issues, as was the creation of uniform laws governing the reinstatement of lapsed clergy.

Tragically, Catholics even persecuted each other. The persecution during the Crusades of Byzantine Catholics by Roman Catholics was among the saddest moments in Christian history. These persecutions occurred for a variety of reasons: ignorance over liturgical and linguistic differences, human greed and jealousy, and cultural and political prejudice. Attempts made over the centuries to heal these wounds repeatedly failed. Pope John Paul II in the early twenty-first century asked forgiveness of Orthodox Church leaders for all historical offenses by Roman Catholics. Some wounds and suspicion remain unhealed.

Part II - Authority's Parallel Systems

The Magisterium

Catholics believe the development of hierarchical structures in the Church is the work of the Spirit. These structures are not revealed in the Bible in an absolutely determined way, but their growth and development are in continuity with biblical revelation. The New Testament clearly states that Jesus called the Twelve to spread the Gospel. They in turn appointed bishops, presbyters, and deacons to assist and to succeed them. These embryonic structures developed over time as the Church responded to diverse cultural and political circumstances. They developed as interdependent ministries held together in a local Church by unity with the bishop and among all the Churches by unity with the Bishop of Rome, successor to the head of the Apostles. Their development is the work of the Spirit who preserves the continuity of faith and communion in the Church. The faithful accept the authority of the ordained as an expression of the Spirit's guidance of the Church. Faith in the teaching authority of the Pope and College of Bishops is in particular a faith in the work of the Spirit leading the Church to the truth of its own being as the Body of Christ.

The Magisterium or teaching authority is a necessary structure for communion of faith. The authority to teach the faith was handed on by Christ to his Apostles who in turn handed it on to their successors, the College of Bishops. Each bishop by ordination is the head of his particular Church, called a diocese, from the Latin word for the place he resides and teaches the faith. Ordination inserts the bishop into the College of Bishops. Each bishop authentically exercises his Magisterium by teaching in communion with the others in the College. The Pope in turn confirms and holds in unity the College of Bishops. The College of Bishops in union with the Bishop of Rome exercises the responsibility to interpret the Catholic Tradition. The Catholic Tradition includes the Scriptures, the sacramental liturgy of the Church, the doctrinal teaching of the College of Bishops, and the experience of the People of God.

It is a living tradition because it is lived and interpreted within varied cultural, political, and historical events. The Catholic Tradition is the way the Gospel of Jesus Christ is lived over time. Cultural, political, and historical events are the context in which the Magisterium interprets the faith of the Church. Changing events inevitably pose new questions for a Gospel way of life and new awarenesses of God's Kingdom manifest in the world. The College of Bishops responds to these events through its teaching, using the Catholic Tradition as its template.

Sacramental and Bureaucratic Structures

Hierarchical authority based in sacramental ordination dates from the first century; bureaucratic forms have accrued over the past twenty centuries. A bishop in charge of a diocese, the territory of a local Church, is called an Ordinary. Ordinaries teach, sanctify and govern the community of believers under their jurisdiction. The bishop of each local Church ordains presbyters to serve the People of God. Ordination does two things. It confers on the priest a share in the priesthood of his bishop and inserts him into the Presbyterate. The presbyters in union with the bishop form one priestly ministry in the local Church. Diocesan priests are ordained to serve a local Church or diocese. They work within the territory of a diocesan bishop and have administrative responsibilities in its parishes and institutions. The bishop ordains deacons to proclaim the

Gospel at the liturgy, but principally through ministries of charity. Bishops also ordain men who are members of religious communities. Religious priests serve under the superior of their communities who may send them to various places worldwide. Religious priests may serve in institutions operated by their communities or in parishes under a local bishop.

Each Ordinary has a curia, or bureaucratic offices, that assist in the exercise of the bishop's ministry to teach, govern and sanctify the faithful. Curial offices, often headed by laity, oversee education, justice issues, missionary activities, personnel, and social services. Lay persons who function in curial offices exercise their tasks under the bishop's authority but do so as bureaucrats or regulators of diocesan activities, not as sharers in his ordination. This difference in the powers and responsibilities of the ordained and the bureaucrats is a source of tension in Church structure. At the same time it offers an opportunity to develop ways of transcending the separation between the ordained and the laity in a particular Church as they function in union with the bishop.

Each diocese has a Finance Council, a Presbyteral Council, and a Judicial Tribunal. The bishop must hear these councils on specific issues before he makes certain final decisions. The bishop gives his juridical authority to the Tribunal, which primarily hears cases for annulment of marriage and declares persons free to marry in the Church. Bishops are encouraged to have a

Pastoral Council made up of laity, religious and clergy to advise on the pastoral concerns of the diocese, but he may function without one.

A diocese is also separated for administrative purposes into geographic regions, called deaneries. Priests are appointed deans by the Ordinary to help him organize the parishes and clergy. Auxiliary bishops serve as helpers to the Ordinary in larger dioceses. By virtue of ordination, an auxiliary functions as a bishop in sacramental celebrations with the faithful, such as confirmation, but more often in administrative roles that are principally regulatory and hence bureaucratic in form. A diocese in a metropolitan area may be designated by the Pope as an Archdiocese and the Ordinary as an Archbishop who has some broader organizational responsibility. He may convene meetings of bishops in his metropolitan area, called a province, to decide such things as how to influence civil legislation that affects the Church and the welfare of society or which priest might be nominated to become a bishop. There are thirty-two provinces of the Roman Rite in the United States and five jurisdictions for Catholics of various Eastern rites, such as the Armenian and Byzantine rites.

Titles in the Church both fascinate and confuse. "Monsignor" is translated as "My Lord" and is the official address when speaking to or of a bishop. In America it is more usual to address a bishop as Your Excellency. Monsignor, more frequently, is a Papal honorary title given to priests in appreciation for Church service or to confer dignity upon a priest currently rendering a special service. This honorary title is usually given at the request of a bishop. There are a host of other titles that have accrued to priests and bishops in various cultures and at differing historical moments. "Eminence" used to be the proper address in Europe for persons of royal blood, but not members of the immediate ruling family. A pope directed it to be used only of Cardinals and it has been so ever since.

Today Cardinals are appointed by the Pope only from among the clergy, but in the past were also appointed from the laity. Cardinals are usually bishops of important metropolitan dioceses or bishops who head the Papal curial offices, but might be leading theologians whom a pope wants to honor. Currently at least one Cardinal is not a bishop but a priest. Only members of the College of Cardinals who are not yet 80 years old may vote in the election of a Pope. The maximum number of those who may cast a vote is currently set at 120. The College of Cardinals is still divided according to the ranks of sacramental ordination as Cardinal, Bishop, Priest or Deacon, yet these designations do not reflect rank by ordination, since almost all are ordained as bishops, but by dignity and rights within the College.

The Pope in International Law is sovereign ruler of Vatican City State, an area of 108.7 acres in the city of Rome. Popes once ruled the Papal States, a far more extensive territory in central Italy. This territory was confiscated by the Kingdom of Italy in 1870. Since

1929, Vatican City and some other parcels of land elsewhere in Italy have been acknowledged as a sovereign state ruled by the Pope. The Bishop of Rome has had a residence in the area of the Vatican hill since the early 500s. There was a Roman cemetery in this area in which the Apostle Peter was buried. A basilica is an important public building, and St. Peter's Basilica was built over his tomb. It is not, however, the Pope's cathedral, a name which designates where the bishop's chair is located from where he teaches. The Pope's diocesan cathedral and residence as Bishop of Rome is on another hill, the Lateran, and is dedicated to St. John.

Why should a Pope be a sovereign ruler? The reasons have changed over the centuries under the influence of various political movements including the feudal system, the divine right of kings, the rise of democracies, the advance of totalitarian governments, and the current development of political and economic world-linking systems. The explanations have included the Pope's status as Vicar of Christ, who is King of Kings and Lord of Lords. For centuries popes wore a triple-crowned tiara that signified authority over all kingdoms. Paul VI gave away his tiara in the 1970s to provide for the poor and the popes have not worn one since. Other reasoning was more pragmatic. During feudal times a pope could only freely function in his office as head of the Church on earth as an independent head of state. Papal teaching later condemned democratic political processes, which in France in the eighteenth and

Germany in the nineteenth century, attacked royal privilege and the Catholic religion. Papal policy continued to insist even into the 1950s that the Catholicism should be established as the State religion where Catholics were the majority. This instruction was given in writing to the Catholic Bishops in the United States as early as the mid-1800s, and the reason was as philosophical as it was political. Only truth and not error must have rights in human societies; Catholicism was the truth and Protestantism was error. The Second Vatican Council in the 1960s changed this official policy and recognized the right of each person to freedom of religious practice. Popes as head of the Church and head of Vatican State continue to send representatives both to the Churches and to the government in almost every country. This ability to speak to governments, societies, and religious bodies gives a pope a unique advantage in influencing global human affairs with the values inherent in the Gospel of Jesus Christ. This may be the most convincing reason for maintaining the Bishop of Rome's headship over a sovereign state.

The Papal Curia

The Papal Curia supports the Pope's universal and immediate pastoral jurisdiction everywhere in the world. It is a large and far reaching organizational system. It includes a Secretariat of State with two branches, one for relationship to local Churches, or dioceses within a country, and another for civil governments, including observer status at the United Nations. The Secretariat maintains a diplomatic corps with embassies or consulates in most nations around the world. There are nine Congregations and thirteen Pontifical Councils, three Tribunals and four Offices, eleven Commissions and Committees and fourteen Institutions within the administrative network of the Roman Curia. Laity, both men and women, religious, and clergy from every nation work in the curial offices in Rome and in embassies throughout the world.

Curial departments, called decasteries, include the Congregation for Bishops. This decastery investigates candidates suggested for episcopal office, gleaned from provincial meetings of bishops under the leadership of an Archbishop, and then nominated by the Papal representative in that country. This allows a review on the reputation of the candidate, as well as his competence for office. The Congregation proposes a name to the Pope who confirms the choice, approves his ordination, and appoints the bishop to his diocese or office. Another decastery, the Congregation for the Causes of Saints, deals with the process of canonizing a person as a saint and considers questions regarding the relics of saints. Canonization means that this person may be petitioned to intercede with God for the good of the Church and is given a place in the liturgical calendar for public liturgy in honor of the saint. Relics are pieces of a saint's body or articles a saint used or touched.

The appointment of bishops and the canonization of saints are exercises in leadership. An episcopal appointment allows a pope to shape the Church for the future through the type of leadership his appointees show in the present. Canonization shapes the way the Church's past is perceived in the present, and thus influences the way Catholics see themselves here and now. There is more to the work of these bureaucratic offices than the tasks they perform, because they help to develop the sense the faithful have of the faith itself. They have another effect, which in some ways shapes the Papacy. By spawning bureaucratic structures in which laity and clergy administer a pope's authority, decasteries have more continuity in their effect on the Church than a pope himself. Popes most often are chosen from among the members of these bureaucracies, while other members continue in office over the rule of several Popes, all the while influencing the life of the Church.

The Sense of the Faithful

No consideration of authority in the Church would be complete without taking into account the sense of the faithful. As the words imply, the faithful have good sense when it comes to their perception of the faith and the communion they share in Christ. This good sense is not self-made, however. It is considered in Catholic Tradition to be a gift of the Spirit, given in Baptism, strengthened in Confirmation, and nourished at the Eucharist. Like the gold coins of which Jesus spoke in parables being given by a king to his ministers, this sense, while God-given, is also something that must be used so that it will bring in a profit, grow, develop and be passed on. The faithful, through liturgical and private prayer, through study of the official teachings of the hierarchy, and by consulting their own expertise can develop a well-formed consciousness of the faith. They grow and develop the sense of the faith that is natural to them as members of the Body of Christ.

Members of a physical organism perceive the health of the whole body and tell the head what it may need to know to care for its members. Similarly, the sense of the faithful is expressed in their attention not only to an understanding and acceptance of what the Magisterium teaches, but also in communicating to the Pope and College of Bishops their own perceptions and concerns about the communion shared in the Body of Christ, and the continuity of the Catholic Faith. This means that the laity not only have the right to address their shepherds but also an obligation in charity to disagree with them when the faith is at stake, and even to correct them when they fail to maintain the communion or the faith. While deference must always be given to the Spirit being at work in the successors to the Apostles, the Spirit of God is given to all the members and can renew the Church by initiating reform among the laity as well as through the Hierarchy.

Vowed Religious

Those in vowed religious life have, through the long history of the religious orders, both co-operated with the authority of the bishops and called them to reform. A religious vocation proceeds from the Spirit's call to intimacy of life with God in communities of common life. A religious vocation is a charismatic way of life based on a call lived out through the traditional vows of poverty, chastity and obedience. These vows enable the religious to live more fully the Gospel of Jesus Christ by renouncing the things of this world in order to live in community with others for the sake of the Kingdom of God. For this reason, the vows of poverty, chastity and obedience are called evangelical or Gospel-based vows.

Religious life is first of all a charism of the laity. It began in the early centuries and grew as persecutions subsided. Lay persons retired to deserted places in Egypt, Syria, Arabia, and other Middle Eastern areas to live the life of hermits or monks. Martin of Tours (d. 397), a Roman soldier converted to Christianity, became a popular bishop and missionary, and founded the first monastery in the west to assist his clergy and himself in their ongoing spiritual development and missionary zeal. Benedict of Nursia is credited with the foundation of religious life in the west around 500, because he wrote the first western monastic rule. He founded the famous monastery at Monte Casino. Like Benedict, religious are members of the laity who gather into voluntary communities of common life and mission. Vowed communities today are separated into those for women and for men. Women religious outnumber men. The majority of male religious communities today have members ordained as priests or deacons. Women religious once had members ordained as deaconesses and may again one day. Deaconesses functioned in eastern cloistered communities and in Roman Catholic communities, like the Carthusian nuns. They proclaimed the Gospel at Mass and provided other services within their communities. Currently, there are discussions in both Orthodox and Catholic circles about once again ordaining women religious as deaconesses.

Charismatic in origin, religious communities are hierarchical in organization. Mixed communities of men and women existed in early Medieval Ireland and in other places. Women who led these communities held authority over both men and women. Abbot is the title given to a leader of an autonomous monastic community of men. Some women in the Middle Ages held the office of Abbess and exercised authority over territory, ordained ministers, and more than one community of women at a time. Their authority was that of a noble woman, as they often were by birth.

An abbot or abbess, following election by the community, receives a liturgical blessing from a bishop to inaugurate the ministry of headship over the community and may serve a life-term. Other religious congregations usually elect their leadership with term limits.

These leaders are given a variety of titles, e.g. provincial, prior or prioress, mother- or father-general, or sister servant.

The most familiar religious communities were founded by very charismatic leaders. Francis of Assisi (d. 1226) created a religious community by insisting on absolute poverty in response to the growing commercialism of northern Italy. His charism was so personal that his many followers found they were unable to live it completely and softened his rule, even before his death. Each community had its own rule of life approved by the local bishop, in which case they were a diocesan community, or by a pope and were exempt from control by the local bishop but nonetheless must cooperate with the Ordinary while working within his diocese. Religious communities, as corporate persons in Canon Law, may hold property, develop their own way of life, and inaugurate their own missions and institutions. This is the way many hospitals, colleges, and other Catholic institutions have been founded over time.

Another religious order, the Jesuits, was founded in 1540 by Ignatius of Loyola, a Spanish nobleman and retired soldier, as the Protestant Reformation swept over Europe, and the lands of the Americas were being developed. Their work in university education was equaled by their missionary activity. Through these ministries they re-evangelized Catholic lands and took the Gospel to pagan peoples. Jesuit influence was so pervasive that they made many enemies and were suppressed by Pope Clement XIV in 1773. They survived only in Russia under Catherine the Great, an Orthodox sovereign. The order was not restored until 1814 by Pius VII. They possessed such successful organizational skills, and had such superior theological and spiritual training that they shaped the rule of life and spiritual practices of many religious communities into the middle of the twentieth century. Following the Second Vatican Council, all religious communities were mandated to return to the original charism of their founders and to refashion their organizational structures and ministries accordingly.

Councils

Councils are perhaps the best example of the integration of the ordained and bureaucratic structures in the Church. Voting membership at Councils has varied over time. In past centuries, theological experts and superiors of religious communities, especially abbots, exercised a vote along with bishops. Today only bishops may vote but theological experts advise them and representatives of other Churches and Christian bodies are invited to observe the sessions. The attendance at Councils has varied widely. Less than three dozen showed up initially when Pope Paul III called for a Council at Trent (1545) to respond to Protestant reformers. Eventually 160 doctors of divinity and around 270 bishops participated. By contrast, the Second Vatican Council attracted around 2,500 bishops. The spread of the Church around the world and improvements in travel have resulted in this growth in participating bishops.

Attendance is not the only thing that has varied widely. The Second Vatican Council held in Rome at St. Peter's Basilica was the twenty-first Ecumenical Council recognized as legitimate by the Catholic Church. Its sessions stretched from 1962-1965. The first Ecumenical Council, held at Nicea in 325, lasted only two months and twelve days, while the sessions of the Council of Trent created the Catholic response to the Protestant Reformation extended over eighteen years from 1545-1563. At least one Council (Basil, 1431) was considered to be Ecumenical only in part. After its first twenty-five sessions it attempted to weaken the powers of the Pope. A Council is legitimate if it has been called by a proper authority and its decrees accepted by the Pope. Constantine called the bishops to Nicea but Pope Sylvester sent legates who presided at the Council and accepted its decrees. Six subsequent Councils in the East are recognized by the Orthodox as well as Catholics. Each was presided over by Papal legates. These Councils were First Constantinople (381), Ephesus (431), Chalcedon (451), Second Constantinople (553), Third Constantinople (680-681), and Second Nicea (787).

A council is ecumenical when it is called to settle issues of doctrine and practice of importance to the universal Church and issues decrees for their solution. Nicea defined the true divinity of Jesus against Arianism and decided the formulation of the date for the celebration of Easter. Ephesus declared that Mary was indeed the Theotokos, God-Bearer, translated in the west as Mother of God. Chalcedon defined that the human and divine natures of Christ are neither mixed nor confused in his one person. The Council of Constance (1414-1418) finally ended one of the most difficult periods in Church history, other than the break between Rome and Constantinople. Constance ended what is known as the Great Western Schism, during which two and even three Popes simultaneously claimed to be the legitimate Bishop of Rome.

Conciliarism is the belief that the supreme authority in the Church is an Ecumenical Council. It was proposed both by theologians scandalized by the Western Schism and by Catholic rulers, some of whom desired to reunite the Church and others who wanted to take advantage of the chaos to gain more power over Church affairs in their own countries. The theory gained wide acceptance among Roman Catholics during the period of the Western Schism. Subsequent to the election of a single legitimate pope, Conciliarism was defined as a heresy. Appeals to a Council against a Pope were forbidden by Pope Martin V in 1418 as contrary to the faith of the Church. An Ecumenical Council is now considered legitimate in the Catholic Church only if it is called by the reigning Pope and its decrees are confirmed by his authority.

The Reformation of course denied papal authority and in contrast emphasized the sense of the faithful.

The Council of Trent countered this emphasis with a clear declaration of the divinely inspired hierarchical nature of the Church. Nevertheless, arguments against papal powers continued to be proposed even within the Catholic Church over succeeding centuries, often at the encouragement of national governments who desired more control of Church affairs within their borders. Vatican I confirmed the supreme authority of the Pope in the Church in 1870 but was unable to complete its work because the Kingdom of Italy seized the Papal States and attacked the Vatican before the Council's conclusion. Vatican II issued a Dogmatic Constitution on the Church which confirmed its hierarchical structure and the authority of the Pope but also balanced these with the collegial nature of the episcopacy and with the universal call to holiness of the entire People of God.

Summary

The structures of authority in the Catholic Church exist for a purpose other than their own continuation. The purpose of the powers of the Bishop in a diocese or the Pope and the College of Bishops in the universal Church is for the sake of the communion of the members and ultimately for the salvation of all humankind. The Hierarchy shares in the Headship of Jesus Christ so that the Church may receive the care of the Good Shepherd and humankind may hear his Gospel, have the means of his saving grace through the sacraments, and experience life in communion with each other in the Church. The structures of authority in the Catholic Church are in service of the plan of God for the sake of the People of God, membership in which is open to all persons through faith.

Authority in the Church expresses the Trinitarian communion of life the members have with each other and deepens that communion. It maintains the faith of the Church as revealed by God in Christ in continuity with the faith of the Apostles. This continuity is not possible without change and development, because the divinely revealed faith is expressed in a human way, expressed in human words and in historical situations. Its human expression can be affected by sinful and corrupt people. Still it is a divine reality, a revelation from God by the power of the Spirit. The Spirit's power is the ultimate reference in any consideration of episcopal or papal authority. Catholicism has been graced with many holy and saintly bishops and popes. The popes in the last century have been exceptional examples of the Spirit's work in the Church. The Spirit works to hold the Church in unity by using the diverse cultural and historical influences that give human expression to the divine revelation and the communion it offers. As Jesus Christ is both true God and true man in one divine person, his Body, the Church, is both a divine reality and human expression in one People of God. Authority in the Church is in the service of this great mystery.

4
The Protestant Reformation

Thousands of books have been written about the need for reform in the Catholic Church that spawned the Protestant Reformation. The Hierarchy was implicated in repeated scandals. Popes and bishops regularly broke their vows of celibacy, lived with women and sired children on whom they bestowed church property and offices. Roman families frequently warred over possession of the Papacy and no less frequently bought their son's election as Pope. The office of Cardinal was sold to make money for popes to enrich themselves or to raise armies to attack Catholic states. Two and even three claimants to the Papacy at a time divided Catholic bishops and theologians, religious and laity. The Hierarchy was populated by the nobility while popes, bishops and abbots controlled enormous amounts of land and wealth. Political and cultural upheaval was raging. The rise of nation states in Europe and their competition for power and resources included attempts by their leaders to capture the Papacy. The French controlled the Papacy for seventy years and moved the Pope's residence to Avignon in France. The Avignon Captivity of the Papacy is an example of the emerging power of nation states. National allegiances were a symptom of a longing to reestablish the cohesion and wealth of the ancient Roman Empire which continued to be the standard for culture in the west. Roman art, literature, architectural skills, world trade, and legal system seemed far superior to the way of life that had succeeded them in feudal societies. Fascination with Greek and Roman philosophies, particularly their definition of human nature, birthed the Renaissance. The renewed interest in the philosophical contribution of the ancients had both compatibility and incompatibility with Christian understandings of the human condition and the divine revelation. Finally, the scientific frame of mind was about to dawn upon Europeans, and Catholic scholars were leading the way. Science trains the mind to look at the world of individual things; Catholic faith gazes upon the things that are and sees their unity. The difference between these scientific and religious points of view was at work in the disagreements between Protestants and Catholics. All of these forces and more swirled together to fertilize the Reformation.

Reformation has but one mother among Catholics. The ultimate reason for ongoing reform is access to and expression of the life of God revealed in Jesus Christ and shared by the Spirit among the members of the

Church. This was the original intent of those Catholic Christians who protested the teaching and practices of the Church in the sixteenth century. The Protestant Reformation began among dedicated members of the Catholic Church. However, from 1520 until the early twentieth century ongoing disputes over doctrine and practice created countless divisions among Christians in the west. The impossibility of reunion by mere human means is apparent from the fact that while the Protestant Reformation had but one mother, it had many fathers.

First among the multiple causes of the Reformation in the western Church was the troubled conscience of believers regarding their access to salvation in Christ. Few of the laity had the opportunity to study their faith. Much of the Church's liturgical practice was laden with superstition. There was no formal curriculum for the education of the clergy. The understanding and practice of the faith for many believers was tentative if not confused. In addition, the members of the Hierarchy did not resist the historical and political pressure to preserve and use their power as an end in itself. Reform was necessary to recall the hierarchical structure to its servant role in the Church's communion. Saintly popes, bishops, priests, religious and laity had repeatedly led reform movements prior to those of Luther, Calvin, and Cranmer. Yet the moral scandals that occurred raised an even more serious question. Could the Pope as head of the Magisterium, the teaching authority in the

Church, be a heretic; and if so, could the Church's faith be preserved? Next, the political and philosophical movements of the time affected the Church's structures and doctrinal formulations. Reformation was needed in the wake of new internal and external forces for change.

True reform begets development of the Church's faith and life. This development is essential to the preservation of the Church's faith in continuity with the Apostles. Alteration makes the Church's faith something other than what God revealed. Vincent of Lerins (d. 450) summarized this distinction a thousand years before the Reformation. He wrote, "Development means that each thing expands to be itself, while alteration means each thing is changed from one thing into another. In the same way, the doctrine of the Christian religion should properly follow the laws of development, that is, by becoming firmer over the years, more ample in the course of time, more exalted as it advances in age." But how to tell development from alteration?

The necessary test of the Spirit's inspiration for any reform in the Church is preservation of the communion of the members, the unity of the one flock under the care of the One Shepherd. Preservation of unity in charity sets development apart from alteration. By its unity the Church most clearly embodies the prayer of Jesus that all may be one as he and the Father are one. The sad truth is the original intent of the Protestant reformers was to return the Church to a purer form of faith and communion. In order to achieve their goal, the reformers rejected Catholic communion under the authority of the Pope as a false representation of the Christian faith and sought to return to what they believed was a more primitive form of the divine revelation and Christian life. The ultimate effect was to create separate Christian bodies that no longer fully expressed Christ's prayer for unity. The Roman counter-reformers sought to preserve both the continuity of the Church's faith and its communion of life in the Catholic Tradition. They were too late to heal the hemorrhage of Roman Catholicism which had so long been in need of reform.

Martin Luther

Catholic theology until about 1200 A.D was created through prayerful contemplation. After 1200, theologians increasingly adopted a scientific method. The original Protestant reformers were traditionalist Catholics but affected by the contemporary scientific mindset. In1520, Martin Luther, a priest and Augustinian monk, publicly objected to the way indulgences were used to bring in cash for the building of St. Peter's Basilica in Rome. Luther's objection was based on his research as a professor of the New Testament. It was the studied opinion of a professional scholar who wanted to maintain continuity with the Catholic faith as it is revealed in the Word of God. Luther declared trade in indulgences offensive to Catholic faith. According to

Scripture, Luther taught, God justified the sinner, and this free gift could be accepted only by faith. Forgiveness of sins was a free gift from God. No one, including the Pope, should profit materially from this gift. Luther went further. No human effort could otherwise achieve this free gift. The Pope's offer of a plenary indulgence troubled the consciences of the people. It led them to believe that their sins were not forgiven in this life, and they would be punished for them in the next life even if they were not damned to hell. They could obtain relief only by some meritorious deed, like a donation to build St. Peter's Basilica. An indulgence given in exchange for a contribution to the Church was not an act of faith but a pious work, which could not earn justification from God who gave it freely to those who believed. Luther's teaching that the forgiveness of sins is a free gift of God and can only be accepted by faith was consistent with the Catholic Tradition, but he moved beyond that tradition in defense of his professional research.

Luther claimed that his faith was solely based on the Bible. However, Luther was influenced not by Scripture alone but also by the prevailing philosophy of William of Occam (d. 1347), a Franciscan friar and Oxford professor. Two hundred years after his death, Occam's innovative thinking continued to have influence on western culture. William of Occam held that God had to be omnipotent in order to be completely free. God's omnipotence could not be proved philosophically. It had to be accepted by faith. Luther interpreted the Scriptures according to Occam's principles. Luther wanted to preserve God's freedom and omnipotence in the justification of sinners. He taught that God freely forgave a sinner through a juridical act. Using the power that belongs only to God, God judged the sinner to be free from the guilt of sin in virtue of the sufferings of Christ. God no longer considered the person's sins. The sinner accepted justification through faith. Faith was trust in God's gift of justice given freely through Jesus Christ. Faith freed the sinner from the fear of damnation to do the good works of love that flowed from this new freedom.

Here Luther introduced a change in Catholic understanding of the human person. He taught that the human will was so corrupted by sin that one was incapable of choosing to do good unless the person was first justified by God. Even after justification a person remained corrupted by sin and unable to do any good that God would reward. Catholic faith taught that human persons, though sinful, were capable of doing good and that God rewarded good behaviors as well as punished evil ones.

William of Occam also championed the power of nation states. Such national states gradually replaced the ideal of a universal Christendom in Europe. Occam believed the Holy Roman Emperor, and by extension all Catholic rulers, had the duty and the authority to depose a heretical Pope. They had this power because princes must defend the Catholic faith and the societies which the faith supported. Luther attacked as heresy the claims of the Pope to grant indulgences in exchange for payment. Neither the Pope nor the Saints could intervene in the judgment of God who was perfectly free and omnipotent. Catholic faith depended only on the Word of God and its effects on the individual conscience. The Pope's claims were heretical, and so the next step for Luther was opposition to the Papacy's claim of authority over the whole Church. He therefore appealed to the Emperor and to Christian princes to counter Papal power in order to preserve the continuity of the Catholic faith. Luther thus severed his communion and that of his reform with the Bishop of Rome. Luther maintained that his reform preserved communion with the Apostolic Church from which the Roman Church had diverged, and that it restored the practices of the Church he identified in the New Testament.

Consequently, he taught that all the faithful shared in the Priesthood of Jesus Christ, who alone was Head of the Church. The ordained were his representatives but the difference between them and the laity was not a difference in the way they shared in Christ, as Head and members. He upheld the baptism both of those old enough to have personal faith as well as of infants, recognizing this had been the tradition of the Church from its beginning. He insisted on the true presence of Christ in the Eucharist because these were Christ's own words to the Church, "This is my body . . . this is my blood." However, Luther rejected the doctrine that the Mass was a sacrifice and the doctrine that explained Christ's real presence in the Eucharist, Transubstantiation.

Transubstantiation was the Catholic explanation of how Christ through the Eucharist gave himself to his Church. As early as 163 A.D., Justin the Martyr taught the Church's faith in the real presence of Christ in the Eucharist. No one could receive until they were baptized. The Spirit transformed the baptized into the likeness of Christ and this likeness was nourished through the Eucharist. The Eucharist must truly be Christ; otherwise the Christian would not be feeding on his or her true likeness. Roman Catholic faith in the real presence of Christ in the Eucharist was based on the power of Christ's words, "This is my body . . . this is my blood," spoken over the elements by the priest. The doctrine of Transubstantiation explained that this faith is not contrary to reason. Around 1250, Thomas Aquinas used Aristotle's philosophy of nature to explain the reasonableness of the Church's faith. Aristotle developed his philosophy 330 years before Christ. He held that all things have a unique substance of their own. Bread's substance is "bread-ness." The fact that bread has texture, flavor, color, and scent is accidental to its "bread-ness" because these can vary but the substance of bread remains. Thomas noted the accidents of bread and wine remained in the Eucharist. One saw and tasted bread and wine. The substance, however, changed by the power of Christ's words to become the body and blood of the risen Lord Jesus. The change was called Transubstantiation. Luther's view of nature was like Occam's; that things are simply what they are in themselves and that there is not such thing as "bread-ness" that can be separated from the taste and texture of bread. Bread and wine remain what they are and do not change. He believed that Christ nevertheless was truly present under these signs. He explained it as "Consubstantiation," because he posited that both Christ and the bread and wine are present. The how he left up to God's omnipotence, but believed because of Christ's words, "My flesh is real food and my blood real drink."

Calvin

It took twenty-five years for the Hierarchy to respond to Luther's reform. By 1545 Protestant reformers multiplied throughout northern Germany, the Netherlands, France, England, and Switzerland. In 1533, John Calvin, a Frenchman living in Switzerland, had a conversion experience. Calvin at twelve had studied for the priesthood and later moved on to study law. After his conversion he joined other Protestant reformers and by 1541, after suffering a number of setbacks, became the leader of the religious and civil reform of the city of Geneva. He was thirty-two. His reform extended Luther's into new areas. Calvin believed all society must be brought into conformity with the Bible as the rule of life. Therefore, he set out to change the political structure in Geneva to a theocracy. The world was corrupt and under the rule of sin. Human society must be brought under the rule of faith and righteousness. The Christian's duty was to build a virtuous character by acting righteously and a virtuous society that supported righteousness. A Calvinist world-view motivated the Puritans to found the New England colonies in the 1600s. Calvinism has continued to play a part in America's culture wars into the twenty-first century.

Calvin's reform followed Luther's in teaching that the sinner is justified by faith alone through grace alone. But Calvin also taught no human actions are capable of any goodness. Without Christian faith, all human actions are positively sinful. Essentially, Calvinism held that the mind and will had become denatured by sin. Human nature was absolutely corrupted. All human actions were evil, even those of believing Christians. God, through the grace of justification, forgave sins and no longer regarded the Christian's actions as sinful, even though there was no good in them. Calvin taught the omnipotent God predestined everyone from all eternity for either heaven or hell. Faith meant more than accepting the grace of justification; it also meant trusting without proof of any kind that God had not damned one to hell. The evidence of this personal faith was the righteous way of life one lived, but this righteousness must be accomplished without doubting God's graciousness.

Calvin sought to reform the fundamental structures of the Church such as the Bible, the Eucharist, and the ordained ministry with the primitive discipline he discovered in the New Testament. Calvin taught that the Scriptures were the rule of faith. The Spirit gives the believer an inner sense to know the truth of the Scriptures, including which books are truly inspired. Calvin's reform, based on ancient historical arguments and supported by the inner sense of the Spirit, reduced the number of books in the Catholic version of the Old Testament by seven plus parts of two others. Calvinism taught that the risen body of Christ was in heaven and could not be received on earth, and therefore denied Christ was really present in the Eucharist. The Spirit made Christ present to the Christian through an inner conviction and hope of joining Christ in the resurrection. Christ was received spiritually in the Eucharist, not in bodily form. The bread and wine were signs that reminded the faithful of Christ's promises, but the bread and wine were not changed. The Mass did not repeat Christ's sacrifice on the cross offered once and for all. Calvin denied the authority of pope and bishop and taught the priesthood of all the believers. He restructured the ordained ministry in keeping with his understanding of the New Testament. The structure was fourfold: pastors, doctors, elders and deacons. Calvinism gave birth to the Reformed Churches. The Presbyterian Church began as the Reformed Church of Scotland. "Presbyterian," taken from the Greek word for elder, signifies that the Church kept presbyters but not episcopoi, or bishops, among their ordained ministers.

Cranmer

Henry VIII influenced the appointment of Thomas Cranmer as Archbishop of Canterbury in 1532. Cranmer helped the King wrest authority over the Church in England from the Papacy. Lands were originally granted to the Church by the nobility to sustain and develop the Church's life and ministries. The Pope and various monastic communities owned and collected annual taxes on great tracts of land in England. Papal taxes supported the Pope's ministry of unity in feudal Christendom. As England changed from an agrarian to a mercantile economy, Papal taxes were a strain on development. The Pope still united Christian Europe against Islamic invasion and in countering Moslem domination of trade with the east, but popes also took sides in disputes among Christian kings. Popes tended to show favor to the kings in France and Spain, because their political and military power could threaten the Papacy. Henry VIII sought equality with these dominant powers.

To assist Henry in his quest, Archbishop Cranmer declared Henry's marriages null, allowing him to remarry in hope of siring a male heir. Together King and Archbishop closed monasteries and confiscated their wealth for the Crown. Cranmer helped quell friction between Catholics and reformers by creating the Book of Common Prayer. In it Cranmer achieved a synthesis of Catholic and newly emerging Reformed perspectives. The Church of England, under his guidance, integrated the Catholic ethos that had been England's heritage with a Reformation independence from Rome that would become its future. Henry had written in defense of the doctrine of Transubstantiation against Luther. He was given the Papal title "Defender of the Faith" because of his book. Cranmer did not deny the real presence of Christ, but in the Prayer of Common Book changed the words of the Catholic Mass to allow a Reformed interpretation of that presence. Cranmer inaugurated the Anglican movement which maintains communion of the Church through liturgical prayer rather than doctrinal statements. His compromise unified England in support of Henry's actions against the Roman Church.

The final break with Rome came later. Cranmer was executed under Queen Mary, Henry's daughter. Mary, a Spanish princess, restored the Catholic Church in England. Elizabeth I, her sister and successor, broke with Rome and established the Church of England under her own authority as Queen. Elizabeth preferred Luther's reform; it was friendlier than Calvinism toward established royal authority and bishops. Elizabeth realized bishops were helpful supports to the Crown and retained them in the Church of England. Years later Calvinism, under Cromwell, led to the beheading of an English King and an Archbishop of Canterbury.

Elizabeth changed little of the Catholic liturgy, pious devotions, and structures of the ministry. English was used in the liturgy rather than Latin to the joy of many. Her reform established a national church independent of Rome but in the Catholic tradition.

Elizabeth implemented a practical political strategy. She managed to unite under her rule the Protestant reformers and the Catholics. Her strategy was to restore the Book of Common Prayer, once again making the liturgy the source of unity for the Church of England. She reinstated to good effect Cranmer's compromise on Transubstantiation. Few English Catholics, especially the clergy, noticed much change, except like the Protestant reformers, Elizabeth allowed for a married clergy. In succeeding centuries as England dominated the seas, world commerce and a vast colonial empire, the Church of England established national churches elsewhere. These national churches formed the Anglican Communion. In some places, the churches in this communion were called Episcopalian, because they retained bishops, *episcopoi*. Episcopal bishops, however, did not retain the same teaching authority as the Catholic College of Bishops. In the Anglican Communion, the teaching authority of the bishops was tempered by the vote of the clergy and laity much like the division of powers found in the Reformed Churches. Catholic in its style, the English reform was Protestant in its content.

The Catholic Counter Reformation

The Council of Trent was convened in 1545 to address the Protestant revolt. Slow in starting, the Catholic response to the Reformation was four hundred years in duration. The Counter-Reformation lasted until the Second Vatican Council (1962). Trent produced multiple reforms. Foremost among them were doctrinal clarifications responding to Protestant claims that the Church had abandoned the ancient Biblical faith. Reforms in discipline, especially of the clergy, responded to the scandals and laxity that Protestant reformers sought to correct. The Council affirmed the Pope as head of the Church whom no power on earth could legitimately depose. The liturgy, especially the creation of a uniform celebration of the Mass, was perhaps Trent's most identifiable reform.

A complete look at the reforms of Trent is not possible here. What follows may assist the non-Catholic to understand Catholic teaching after Trent. The Council of Trent was more optimistic than the Protestants about sinful human nature. God made all thing good. Sin did not make all human works evil. The human will was created free by God. Its freedom is the will's capacity to be moved by God. Human works were good or evil depending on the intent of the person and the moral content of the action. Still all human beings are sinners in need of redemption. The Word of God was incarnated in Jesus through whom God intended all be redeemed. Redemption was accomplished for all by

Christ's death and resurrection, but must be personally accepted by faith as justification, the forgiveness of sins. Human nature, even though justified by faith, is still weakened by sin's effects. Justification does not end with the forgiveness of sins. Justification begins the transformation by which the person shares in the life of God. This transformation is not complete until it is fulfilled in heaven. Grace is the life of God shared; it is the free gift of God. Sin has weakened the believer's ability to respond fully to God's grace. The sinner can respond to God because grace prepares and assists the response. Grace is at work bestowing the gift of faith and assisting the believer to persevere in faith until it is accomplished in heaven. The believing Christian may sin and need the grace of forgiveness. Ongoing repentance is necessary during life's graced journey. Grace is at work even in the reward the person receives from God. The faithful are credited by God's free gift for all their efforts to respond to God's grace in their lives. They are by God's condescension co-workers in their own redemption, which is God's gift to them.

Optimistic about human nature and salvation, Trent was pessimistic about salvation outside the Catholic Church. Trent decreed that there is no salvation without the Church. Luther proposed that the Church is the spiritual communion of the faithful. Trent taught that the Church was the incarnate presence of Christ in the world. His Headship was exercised by the ministry of the pope and bishops. Communion with Christ and his Church was not possible without communion with the College of Bishops in union with the Bishop of Rome. They alone were entrusted with Christ's teaching, governing and sanctifying authority. The means necessary for salvation were found in the Church's sacraments, administered by the Bishops and their priests for the justification and sanctification of the faithful. Baptism forgave all one's sins, conferred a share in the life of the Trinity and imparted the gift of faith through which the baptized know God. Baptism was necessary for salvation for all who have come to believe in Christ. It was questionable whether the non-baptized could be saved. One had to at least desire baptism to be saved. Transubstantiation was the doctrine of the Church and must be believed. Christ was truly present, but his presence was not such that his flesh could be torn or suffer. The Eucharist was an unbloody sacrifice. What was once and for all offered on the cross was offered to God at each Mass. The repetition of this sacrifice did not mean that Christ died again and again. The Church was given his one sacrifice to offer throughout time, declaring his death until he comes again in glory. All the baptized have a share in the Priesthood of Christ and can offer themselves with him in the sacrifice of the Mass. However, his sacrifice can only be offered for the faithful by the ordained, who share in Christ's Headship and so in his High Priesthood.

The Council of Trent reformed the laxity of the Church that the Protestants decried. All priests were to be educated in seminaries with episcopal oversight of their curriculum. Philosophical and theological studies were prescribed by Rome, which also mandated strict spiritual formation in prayer and personal discipline. Each parish was to erect a school; religious education of children and adults was to take place on a regular basis. Preaching was mandated at every Sunday Mass. Communities of religious men and women were to strictly reform their rule of life and remove all worldly abuses.

Bishops must be resident in their diocese and care for their people by regularly visiting parishes and institutions. Holy things, including indulgences, could not be purchased in order to achieve their spiritual effects. Catholic governments must not interfere in the affairs of the Church or claim powers that belong solely to the pope and the bishops. Where the government was Catholic, it must support the Church and not give freedom to Protestants to spread their heresy. Where the government was not Catholic, members of the Church must insist on the right to practice their faith and to have full citizenship. These reforms, not implemented everywhere with the same vigor, were nonetheless emphasized and expanded with varying degrees of success over the next four hundred years.

The most identifiable contribution of Trent is the reform of the Mass. Multiple liturgical forms were available prior to Trent. Multiple forms continued only among eastern Catholics and in a few religious orders (for example, the Carthusians and the Dominicans). The structure of the Roman Mass was made uniform at Trent. The Mass of the Roman Rite was the Church's response to the Protestant Revolt. The arrangement of the altar, the purity of the bread and wine, the content of beeswax in the candles, and the placement of the tabernacle proclaimed the doctrine of Transubstantiation and the sacrificial nature of the rite. All the actions of the Mass must be performed by the ordained. The words were repeated exactly by each priest. The actions or rubrics, because they were printed in red, were performed without variation. The faithful exercised their priesthood through spiritual participation as they watched the drama of salvation unfold in the ritual. The Word of God was proclaimed in unchanging Latin, not the language of the people. Musicians, choir, and lay acolytes assisted the essential action of the ordained priest, who offered the sacrifice of Christ. The faithful received communion under the form of bread only, as had been the custom since about 1000. The cup was reserved to the priest, despite centuries of agitation in the Church for its restoration to the faithful. All of these reforms emphasized the sacred character of the liturgy. They also emphasized the difference in the share the ordained had in the Priesthood of Christ. The Tridentine Mass embodied the Catholic Counter-Reformation and safeguarded the unity of the Catholic Church in its opposition to Protestantism.

Summary

The reform of Trent was badly needed. Catholics had been crying out for comprehensive reform for centuries before Martin Luther. His reform and the other Protestant movements split the Church in the west but catalyzed a thorough internal reform of the Catholic Church. This reform took place just as European Christians were beginning to colonize the western hemisphere, Asia, and Africa. The divisions between Protestants and Catholics spread to all these lands. Terrible wars and carnage in Europe, not only between Catholics and Protestants but also among Protestant sects, raged for two centuries. The legacy of these struggles encouraged the secularization of western cultures and the development of materialist economic systems, both capitalist and communist. Yet over the centuries these reform movements also broke new spiritual ground.

Ongoing reform movements, both Protestant and Catholic, renewed prayer and personal devotion among Christians. Catholics and Protestants founded new schools and universities. Scripture study and historical research took on new life. New religious orders multiplied in the Catholic Church, enriching and expanding its spiritual life and mission outreach. The Protestant reform encouraged democracies, and Catholic thought helped develop democratic theory. Luther's insistence on the power of faith to bring healing to the conscience became integral to self-help movements in the twentieth century, replacing the addict's self-condemnation with God's judgment of forgiveness. The Catholic Church was forced to integrate its teaching with modern scientific theory. Tragedies as diverse as the treatment of Galileo and witch-hunts mark this transition. Nevertheless, the Catholic integration of faith and science eventually included advances in genetic research by a Catholic monk, the development and use of international radio, medical research and the advancement of modern medical procedures by Catholic religious women, and the development of ethical thought on issues like war, poverty, medicine, justice, capital punishment, unions, economics, international relations, and human rights at every stage of life.

5
The Second Vatican Council

Pope John XXIII called the Second Vatican Council in 1962 to address developments in modern life and the world order. In less than fifty years there had been two world wars followed by the threat of the total nuclear destruction of the earth. Modern communication had supported the rise of totalitarian regimes; the cold war was raging. The European colonial system, which a century before had ended in South America, was beginning to break up in Africa and Asia. Satellites were circling the earth; modern technical advancements and mass communication were changing the political and economic landscape. The world had entered a new social order.

Previously, Pope John shocked his Curia by addressing a formal letter, an encyclical, not in the traditional way to the College of Bishops or to all the faithful, but to "all men of good will." *Peace on Earth* appealed to the same audience as the angels at

Bethlehem had proclaimed Christ's birth. Peace on earth was possible, the Pope wrote, if the earth and its resources were justly shared. John issued another encyclical, *Mother and Teacher*, to the members of the Church. The Church has a message that it must not keep for itself, but is commissioned by Christ to address to the whole world. This commission's success depends on the Church's ability to discern the times. Pope John called upon the whole human community to make the peace Christ brings real among peoples and nations. He called upon the members of the Church to bring about a renewal within the Church's life so that they could share Christ's life with the world. The Pope called the Council to address the ways in which the Church would share Christ's life with the world into the twenty-first century.

In December 1963, over two thousand bishops at the Second Vatican Council issued the first two of sixteen documents, the *Constitution on the Sacred Liturgy* and the *Decree on the Means of Social Communication*. These two documents addressed both the members of the Catholic Church and the citizens of the global community, signaling the Council's intent to communicate the Gospel anew within the Church and modern society. The liturgy communicates divine life to the People of God. Modern means of communication enlivened or enslaved societies, developed human life, or brought about its destruction. Beginning with its own liturgical life, the Church was ready to address the whole of modern humankind concerning the mystery of God's self-revelation in Christ.

The Tridentine Mass was a sixteenth century view of Church worship. Nineteenth and twentieth century research proved that more ancient forms and practices were the historical norm. The ancient forms held promise for communicating the richness of Catholic Eucharistic faith in modern times. The *Constitution on the Sacred Liturgy* was the fruit of that research. The Council's most important liturgical renewal was the reintroduction of the full participation of the faithful in the Mass. It also re-emphasized the variety of Christ's presence: in the assembly, in the priest presider, in the Word of God, and most particularly in the Eucharistic Prayer and reception of communion. As the laity regained their part in liturgical prayer, they were encouraged at every Mass both to proclaim the Word of God and to receive Holy Communion, even from the cup. Renewed themselves in Christ's life, the faithful were to be in dialogue with the world, there to share the life of Christ. Those who celebrated the liturgy were to take the lead in social communication. Social communication was itself conceived in Eucharistic terms as the sharing, not just of data, but of persons in the human community, not the manipulation of information, but the giving of oneself in service for the sake of the world.

At the conclusion of its second session in November 1964, Vatican II produced the *Dogmatic Constitution on the Church*, the *Decree on the Catholic Eastern*

Churches, and the *Decree on Ecumenism*. These three documents reoriented the Church in its relation to itself and to separated Christian Churches and bodies. The *Dogmatic Constitution* declared that all the members of the Church are called to holiness. This universal call to holiness was one of the most important contributions of the Council to the renewal of Catholic spiritual life. All the members shared the life of the Trinity in one communion of life. As such the Church constitutes one People of God. Access to and expression of the life of God, revealed in Christ and shared by the Spirit, is open to all, clergy and laity. The call to and means of holiness are universal in the Church. All the faithful share in the divine transformation of life. The hierarchical structure of the Church is by God's design at the service of all the members attaining the holiness of God.

The hierarchically structured Church is composed of the College of Bishops in union with the Pope, priests who share in the priesthood of their bishop as one Presbyterate, deacons who assist the bishop in the works of charity, and the laity who sanctify themselves and the world by expressing communion with Christ in their lives and in their work. The religious orders are gathered from the laity and the ordained. They are men and women assembled into communities either of consecrated life, who dedicate themselves to prayer for the Church and the world, or of apostolic life, who prayerfully carry on the mission of the Church in the world.

The document on the Church and the *Decree on the Pastoral Office of Bishops in the Church*, issued a year later, clarify the relationship of the College of Bishops to the Pope. Bishops by ordination share the same high priestly powers and are inserted into the College of Bishops, who are the successors to the Apostles. Bishops are heads of local Churches and not the local representatives of the Pope but his brother bishops. The Pope by virtue of his office as Bishop of Rome is the center of unity for the College of Bishops, and for this reason is endowed with universal jurisdiction in the Church and with the sole right to appoint or confirm the appointment of Bishops. The teaching authority in the Church, the Magisterium, is held by the College of Bishops in union with the Pope. This authority is infallible when invoked as such in a specific way by the Pope or when the consistent teaching of the members of the College on a specific matter expresses its gravity.

The Eastern Catholic Churches suffered from the Catholic Counter-Reformation's insistence on conformity to Papal authority and Roman practices. They were in danger not only of losing their ancient heritage to this Roman control but also of not being able to pass on their traditions to the many émigrés from their territories that had moved into areas in the west dominated by Roman Catholics. Many of the Middle Eastern and Eastern European immigrants to America were unable to celebrate their Eastern Catholic traditions, especially with regard to their married clergy. The *Decree on the Catholic Eastern Churches* restored the rights of the Eastern Patriarchs to rule their Churches, including the right to appoint bishops within their own territories. It also confirmed the use of their ancient liturgical forms. By this decree the equality of the Eastern and Roman traditions was renewed.

The *Decree on Ecumenism* recognized that the Orthodox Churches embodied the continuity of the Apostolic Faith, including the apostolic succession of their bishops and the validity of their sacramental life. Only their lack of communion with the Bishop of Rome kept them from being one with the Catholic Church. Union with the Orthodox has been the goal of popes since the Council. The reference to other ecclesial or church bodies in the document refers to those churches which express elements of the revelation of Jesus Christ but do not fully express continuity of faith, structure, and sacramental life in the Apostolic tradition. The Catholic Church has pursued union with these primarily Protestant bodies through a variety of means, especially doctrinal dialogues. These dialogues have resulted in some cases in agreement on significant issues which originally divided Protestants and Catholics. Lutherans and Catholics have issued joint statements of agreement on justification and grace, the real presence of Christ in the Eucharist, and salvation by faith. Significant issues still are being discussed. Protestant Churches held significant liturgical discussions among themselves and with Catholic and

Orthodox Churches on Baptism, Eucharist and Ministry. Various Protestant Churches have reintroduced liturgical forms abandoned at the time of the Reformation. These include the triple ranks in the ordained ministry of bishop, presbyter and deacon, as well as more regular reception of communion on Sundays, the anointing of the sick, and even the penitential use of ashes.

At the close of the Second Vatican Council in fall of 1965, the Bishops issued ten final documents. Among these was the *Declaration on Religious Liberty* which ended the Church's siege mentality left over from the Reformation, and declared the right of persons to seek God without civil or religious constraint. The Declaration does not hold that all ways to God are equal. The Catholic Church holds that Jesus Christ is God's full and unique self-revelation and that this revelation is fully available only in the Catholic Church. However, human nature is created by God with a necessary, uniquely personal, and inalienable freedom to pursue God. This pursuit of God may not be restricted by any person, civil government, or religious body. The Council's statement on religious liberty was a reflection on the Church's experience in the United States and other countries where religious liberty had been guaranteed for two centuries, even at times in the face of papal opposition. The Council did not decide how freedom of conscience was to operate within the Church. Nor did it determine how the obligation to seek and live truth, which is the duty of every person, was to be exercised in regard to its own doctrinal statement that the truth of divine revelation is to be found in its fullness only in the Catholic Church. These questions have continued to be debated in the Church. Pope John Paul II took special care during his twenty-five year pastorate to address these issues of freedom of conscience and the duty to pursue truth.

The *Pastoral Constitution on the Church in the Modern World* reshaped the Catholic Church's response to the wider human community. The Constitution used a pastoral rather than doctrinal approach to contemporary issues. The Council reflected on the world's circumstances and spoke eloquently of the Gospel and the light it shed on the human condition. Its title in Latin, *Gaudium et Spes* or "Joy and Hope," captured the intent of the document which recently has been called overly optimistic. The bishops who assembled at the Council had guided the Church through world wars and religious persecution by totalitarian regimes, gazed with the rest of humankind into the abyss of nuclear holocaust, and stood with their flocks in third world countries against colonialism and economic domination by first world businesses and banking systems. The Gospel sustained them through all of these circumstances. They had good reason to hope that, if it was given to the world in mutual dialogue, the Gospel may well sustain the planet. The Council appealed to the essence of God's revelation in Christ, solidarity with the human situation, as the path for the Church in the modern world.

The other eight documents the Council issued included the one on pastoral office of bishops mentioned above and two on priests, one on their training and another on their life and ministry. There has been a consistent effort to expand the formation of the clergy since the Council, notably by John Paul II in the 1990s. The *Dogmatic Constitution on Divine Revelation* implemented the research on Scripture introduced by Protestant scholars in the nineteenth century. In 1948 Pope Pius XII finally granted permission for such research to Catholics. Catholic scholarship rapidly gained peership with its Protestant forerunners. The document inaugurated a new era in Scriptural prayer and study for Catholics. They had previously been restricted from using the Bible privately, for fear that they would succumb to Protestant interpretations. New opportunities opened for dialogue with Protestant Christians, especially among lay Catholics. The *Decree on the Laity* advanced their role in the evangelization of the contemporary world and thus fulfilled the promise of the *Dogmatic Constitution on the Church*. The *Declaration on Christian Education* implemented the Council's teaching at all stages of catechesis and faith formation. One aspect of Christian education changed by the Council was the age-old condemnation of the Jews implicit in the Church's own Holy Week liturgy prior to the Council and in many of its historical documents.

In its *Declaration on the Relation of the Church to Non-Christian Religions,* the Council taught respect for all world religions and asked for reconciliation with Islam over past conflicts, as well as mutual future cooperation for the sake of all humanity. The Council condemned all forms of anti-Semitism and declared:

> Even though the Jewish authorities and those who followed their lead pressed for the death of Christ, neither all Jews indiscriminately at the time, nor Jews today, can be charged with the crimes committed during his passion. It is true that the Church is the new people of God, yet the Jews should not be spoken of as rejected or accursed as if this followed from holy Scripture.

Since Vatican II, Catholic popes, bishops and theologians have engaged in ongoing discussions with Jewish religious leaders. Forty years after the Declaration, its content is not well known in the State of Israel, and scholars continue to work out the knotty diplomatic issues between the Vatican and Israel.

The Second Vatican reinvigorated the Catholic Church, making it more truly itself in the modern world. Life in the modern world has become more complex since the Council, but its work continues to guide the Church in continuity with its own Apostolic Faith. Hundreds of developments in the life of the

Church and its relationship with other religious groups, governments, and public service concerns continue to be directed by the teaching of the Council. Pope Paul VI succeeded John XXIII and oversaw the sessions of the Council. He issued many of the documents which implemented the Council's reforms. John Paul II, during his twenty-five years as Pope, issued many encyclicals and letters of instruction, clarifying and continuing the work of the Council in which he had participated as a young bishop. As issues develop in the life of the Church and the world, there will inevitably be a need to call another Ecumenical Council. Until then, the Second Vatican Council will continue to be studied and integrated into the life of the Church.

6
The Uniqueness of the Catholic Church

The Second Vatican Council dismantled many of the Church's defenses against Protestantism and modernity. Perhaps in part because of this, the question most frequently asked today is, "What makes the Catholic Church unique among other Christian denominations?" The Church claims a unique status among world religions and in particular among other Christian bodies. In relation to world religions, the Catholic Church claims that the fullness of God's saving revelation is available only through Christ and his Catholic Church. But this divine revelation is not an exclusive possession of the Church. It is a treasure meant to be shared among all peoples for their salvation. Nor does the Church condemn those who are outside its membership. The Church honors the revelation of God in creation and God's particular presence to persons who seek God with a sincere heart. The Church teaches that other Christian bodies have elements of the divine revelation, but not the fullness of God's saving revelation in Christ available in the Catholic Church's teachings and communion of life. The Church intends this claim as a means of unity among Christians rather than as a mark of exclusion. The Church's mission is to unite Christians in a practical way with each other and the whole human race with God. The Church's unique status is an expression of its mission. The Church must be catholic or universal in the means to salvation it offers if it is to accomplish its divine mission. It must also be universal in its membership.

Cyril, the Bishop of Jerusalem (d. 386), said the Church calls itself Catholic because it contains persons from every class and the means of salvation for them all. G. K. Chesterton (d. 1936) defined Catholic as "here they all come." Andrew Greeley adds "and they are bringing everything with them." The Catholic Tradition unites a marvelous diversity of viewpoints, cultures, and tensions in its long history, current membership, and ongoing life. Most Catholic parishes are more ethnically and economically diverse than comparable Orthodox or Protestant congregations. The same is true of Catholic dioceses as compared with other Christian judicatories. The Catholic Church is, as Tertullian (d. 225) said, present in every nation and culture but does not claim any one as its own. Rather, the Church's mission is to gather all of these to God. The

Spirit gives the Church the means to gather all persons to God in Christ. They are its liturgy and sacraments, its authentic teaching of the Word of God, the witness to God's holiness in its members' lives, prayer, and works of justice and charity, and its hierarchical structure which embodies the Shepherding of Christ and mirrors the life of the Trinity. This complete presence of God's self-revelation in Christ is one of the reasons the Catholic Church believes it is entitled to call itself Catholic or universal in its faith, teaching and practice.

One of the traditional dividing points among Christians is whether the Catholic Church maintained continuity of faith with the preaching of Jesus and his Apostles. The Catholic answer is that faith has an intelligible content but the Church is not simply a set of intellectual propositions. The Church is a way of life lived together binding members both to God and to each other in Christ. The Catholic Church is the Church founded by Jesus through the ministry of his Apostles, and it is the historical Church from which other Christian bodies separated. When a Christian who was baptized elsewhere comes into full communion of the Catholic Church, he or she comes into full communion with the life of Christ lived in this world.

The Catholic Church's unique historical status does not mean its members are without fault or failing. The Church lives in the world and is subject to its sinful conditions. At times its members and leaders fail heinously in the practice of its faith and teachings. As a consequence, like other world religions, the Catholic Church has a bad reputation for acrimonious relations with other religions and even other Christians. The four hundred years between the Council of Trent and the Second Vatican Council are marked by polemics stressing the differences between Catholics and Protestants. The same can be said since the split a thousand years ago between Catholic and Orthodox Churches. Catholic statements addressing these divisions may appear to define reconciliation and reunion as a one-sided submission to an authority that cannot be trusted. But the Church believes that in its Head, Jesus Christ, it shares in the Holiness of God for the sake of the unity for all. Among all Christian bodies, the Catholic Church offers the best means for practical unity. The last several popes recognized that success in Christian unity is the sign the world needs to foster real unity in the human community at large. Reunion among Christians is the necessary ministry of the Catholic Church in our time, if it is to be true to its name, its mission, and the prayer of its Head, Jesus Christ, that all may be one as he and the Father are one.

The Catholic and Orthodox Churches

What today are the Orthodox Churches were once united with the Church of Rome as one Catholic Church east and west. The eastern Catholic tradition influenced the formulation of the early creeds, the doctrinal teachings concerning the Trinity, Christ's divinity and humanity, Mary's Motherhood of God, and the sacramental liturgy and theology of the Church, and the Magisterium. Pope John Paul II (d. 2005) said the Church needs once again to breathe the Spirit of God with both its lungs, its eastern and western traditions. It is true that the Catholic Church has preserved unity with some of the eastern Churches, but the majority of eastern rite Christians are members of the Orthodox Churches. Only when the Catholic Church has reestablished practical union with them will the One, Holy, Catholic, and Apostolic Church be fully expressed as it was in the first centuries. The New Testament was written and passed on by the Apostles and their successors within that one Church. The essential first creeds and doctrines were developed by the one Church at seven Ecumenical Councils that span the first five centuries of its life. Like the Catholic Church, the Orthodox Churches have preserved the same Scriptures, sacraments, and church structure that is apparent in the writing and practices of the first generation of successor-bishops to the Apostles. Both Orthodox and Catholics have preserved the continuity of their faith through a Magisterium exercised by their bishops.

While the Orthodox Churches preserve the Catholic Tradition, they have not succeeded in preserving either practical unity among themselves or unity with the Church in the west. The Catholic Church is in a unique position to contribute a ministry of unity exercised by the Bishop of Rome. His ministry developed over centuries in response to internal and external forces that divided local Churches and limited the ability of their bishops to preserve practical unity with each other. However, Rome has a history of centralizing authority and of not honoring the autonomy of the eastern Patriarchates. The Orthodox, in accepting the Pope's ministry of unity, risk the autonomy of their bishops and Patriarchs. Rome's solution to this risk is to restructure the way the Pope exercises his ministry and make it more respectful of the long tradition of Patriarchal leadership in the Orthodox Churches. Restructuring which began in the period since the Second Vatican Council in regard to the Eastern Catholic Churches must now be applied to relations with the Orthodox. Orthodoxy, on its part, must both allow for the development of doctrine as the continuing work of the Spirit in the Church and decide how a Papal ministry of unity might be expressed in continuity with its long and venerable tradition.

How do the development of doctrine and the Papal ministry work together for unity in the Church? Jesus asked his disciples, "Do you understand what I have told you?" Receiving their positive response, he went on to say, "Then you are like a wise householder who can bring forth from his storehouse things both new and old." The development of doctrine is the fulfillment of his words and is essential to the Church's ability to bring forth both the new and the old. Development is the way the faith remains the same while becoming more truly itself. Unfortunately, the Catholic Church has not clarified what the requirements are for true development versus alteration. Reform in language and practice is essential to handing on the faith in its entirety, but it must also be demonstrated that new formulations and practices hand on the same faith and not an alteration. The demonstration that the early Church's faith was in continuity with that of Abraham and Moses was essential to the early proclamation of the Gospel. In every age, confirming the continuity of the Church's faith and practice with that of the Apostolic Church has been the chief duty of the Magisterium. In each instance development demands reformulation, but by what criteria is its reformulation to be judged authentic? The answer is uniquely present in the interplay between the Pope's ministry of unity and the authority of an Ecumenical Council. The Bishop of Rome as the Vicar of Peter accepts the deliberations of his brother bishops in council and affirms them. This interplay continues the gift Jesus (Luke 22:32) conferred on Peter when he said, "I have prayed for you, Peter, that your faith may never fail. You in your turn must strengthen your brothers." The development of doctrine fulfills Christ's promise when it is affirmed as authentic in the communio of the College of Bishops in union with the Pope. *Communio*, however, does not mean uniformity.

The maxim for Catholic life has always been "unity in essentials and diversity in all else." The

Church, united east and west, has believed the same faith but expressed that faith in diverse theological formulations and liturgical practices. This diversity, once a source of suspicion and division, has become since Vatican II a source of renewal for Catholics. The eastern Catholic Tradition focused on the work of the Holy Spirit and on "divinization," God's transforming humankind in the divine likeness. The east described divinization as sharing God's "energies" or "emanations." The west had a different theological focus but the same faith. Roman Catholicism spoke of sharing the divine nature through grace. Graces were named according to the function each performed. Sanctifying grace made a person capable of God's holiness. Actual grace moved the person to act in response to God. However, since Vatican II, Roman Catholics have re-emphasized the ancient Christian writers (the Fathers of the Church) and western mystical theology. These sources reprise the mystical focus of eastern Catholicism, especially attention to the Spirit and divinization. This re-emphasis fostered a renewed appreciation among Roman Catholics of the Church's theological diversity. Similarly, there has been a renewal of liturgical life in the west because of dialogue with Catholic Byzantine and Oriental traditions.

The Roman Rite allows only unleavened bread at the Eucharist. In the Eastern rites leavened bread is used. Yet the faith of the one Church since the earliest centuries is in the real presence of Christ in the

Eucharist. The east emphasizes Christ's presence as the work of the Spirit and the west as the result of Christ's words spoken over the elements of bread and wine. Still both believe that the whole Christ, body and blood, humanity and divinity, Head and members, is received by the communicants. The reason for this common faith in the Eucharistic presence of Christ is that Catholics both east and west believe Christ humbled himself to share in our humanity so that he could share with us his divinity. The members must be fed on the real person of Christ because they are being transformed into his likeness. Since Vatican II, the Roman liturgy emphasizes the invocation of the Holy Spirit upon the bread and wine and upon the people in its Eucharistic Prayers. The renewal of this ancient liturgical practice makes Roman Catholics more appreciative of eastern Catholicism's contribution to their shared liturgical practice. This is another example of the way one faith is professed but may be explained and celebrated by diverse means. The great concern of the Catholic Church, east and west, is that one faith be expressed by the diverse means employed.

Catholics and Protestants

Protestant Churches vary not only in means of expression but in the faith they express. In dialogues with various Protestant bodies, Catholics seek to clarify the faith diverse practices express. In dialogues with the Lutheran and Anglican Churches, Catholic theologians have reached agreement on many of the doctrinal formulations that originally separated these bodies from Rome. While different emphasis is still apparent, Catholics and Lutherans agree on salvation by grace through faith, on the centrality of the Word of God, and on the real presence of Christ in the Eucharist. Lutherans and Catholics are divided over the effects of sin on the human condition and on the Church's authority structure. Anglicans and Catholics are also divided over issues of authority and the magisterium. The Catholic Church continues to question the validity of Anglican and Lutheran ordinations. At the same time new issues have arisen, such as the ordination of women by some Lutheran and Anglican Churches. Ordination of women now divides them within their own communions and from the Catholic Church. What makes the position of the Catholic Church unique in these dialogues is that Lutherans and Anglicans continue in large measure to maintain the faith and practices of the Catholic Church.

The Catholic Church also remains the template for Protestants who have rejected its teachings and practices. The faith of Reformed Churches in the Trinity and their adherence to the Scriptures continues to be in the Catholic Tradition. However, their insistence that the Catholic Church broke with the faith of the Apostles, as Reformed Christians discern it in the New Testament, is a remnant of a sixteenth century view of history. The period of the Reformation coincided with the beginnings of a scientific view of the world. The Reformed movement initiated what they believed to be a scientifically historical investigation of the Bible and Church history. The goal of Protestant historical investigation was to prove that the Catholic Church had diverted from New Testament religion. What developed over the last four centuries was a thorough questioning of the sources of the Bible and of Church history. In some instances historical research created profound skepticism. Did Jesus actually say the things recorded in the Bible? Did he intend to found a Church? In other instances, historical research showed diverse New Testament practices existed side by side and were gradually unified by consensus among leaders. Development was taking place in the Church's doctrine and forms of governance from the beginning. A New Testament Church is not distinguishable from the Catholic Church, nor did the Catholic Church develop later and supplant the Church of the original disciples. Scientific investigation indicated that the Reformed movement, which developed a great tradition of thoughtful theological engagement with the Bible, had lost its original intellectual reason for existence as a separatist movement.

It remains to be seen whether the Reformed Churches still have another reason for being. Their continued existence questions the Catholic Church about its own internal continuity of faith and practice. Have Catholics sufficiently dealt with the question of freedom of conscience within the Church? The last Ecumenical Council reformed the relationship between the Pope and College of Bishops. Does the next Ecumenical Council need to reform episcopal governance and include the laity in some real way, other than bureaucratically? Perhaps the Reformed movement which continues to express these concerns has a place within the Catholic Church at last and not simply outside it.

Catholics and Jews

Much of the theology of the Catholic Church and many of its practices come from its Jewish roots. Baptism and the laying on of hands were Jewish rituals used by Jesus and his disciples. Jewish notions of angels and demons were carried into Catholic practice.

Some from the Jewish priestly cast became Christians. Their influence was felt early on in the Church's faith and practice, as witnessed in the Letter to the Hebrews. A bishop's miter and skull cap recall the high priest's miter and the Jewish worshiper's yarmulke. The dialogue responses used in synagogue worship are used in Catholic liturgy. The ancient custom of greeting the congregation with shalom, "peace be with you," is used by a bishop as he begins Mass. The Eucharistic Prayer at Mass begins with a Jewish dialogue between the presider and congregation declaring "the Lord be with you" and inviting the assembly to "lift up your hearts." Jewish temple worship, recorded in the Torah and interpreted by scholarly rabbis, influenced Catholic liturgical practices in the Middle Ages, especially church liturgical design. Concentric interior elements, such as the choir screen, Rood screen and communion rail designating increasingly more sacred space, mirrored the design of the Jerusalem Temple with its outer and inner courts and tabernacle at its center. At the center of the sacred architecture, the tabernacle of the Temple held the Ark of the Covenant; the Catholic tabernacle held the reserved Eucharist. Jewish scholarship in Biblical theology and ethics also greatly influenced Catholic thought and practice beginning with the teachings of Christ.

Jesus, a Jewish rabbi, taught the importance of prayer joined to fasting and almsgiving, and his very Jewish teaching (Matthew 6) is proclaimed every Ash Wednesday at the beginning of Lent. Among Christ's teachings (Matthew 5:25-26) is the Jewish belief in "Purgatory." Purification is essentially a Jewish belief carried into Catholicism by the first disciples. Purification is based on the Jewish faith in the holiness and justice of God. The holiness of God demands that one must be completely purified in heart and mind before coming into God's presence. Jesus described a person who had not settled a conflict with a neighbor being turned over to the judge and thrown into prison until the last penny of the debt was paid. The justice of God is saving and does not condemn a person who has striven to respond to God's promises and grace, but the justice of God does demand complete conversion of heart and mind, purification. Paul (1 Corinthians 3:10-15) describes how this divine purification will test the Christian's works. When he comes again, what each has built on Christ's firm foundation will be tested as if by fire. What is precious will be further purified and what is dross will be burned up. Persons will escape this fire as if from a building in which they were living, one they built in the Lord. *Revelation* offers multiple images of Christ purifying the Churches and even the whole universe at his coming. Early Catholic Christians developed this Jewish understanding of God's work through Jesus Christ and looked forward to God completing their purification so they might be able to look upon the face of God. Unfortunately, many preachers have confused Catholic doctrine with popular images used in the Bible. Purgatory, according to Catholic doctrine agreed upon by the Church both east and west, is not a place or a period of time or even a physical fire. It is the promise that God's grace will complete, albeit through painful recognition of one's sinfulness, the work of conversion and purification that God has begun in the sinner.

Jewish influence on Catholic ethics is profound. Judaism developed the ethos of the covenant, which draws all human action into personal relationship with God, the Faithful One. In the Jewish ethical tradition, the Holiness of God is to be shown by compassion. The love of God, the great commandment, binds persons together in human community through personal acts of kindness. In these communities persons are understood to be transcendent beings whose value is more than their productivity. Catholic moral theology further developed this Jewish perspective in light of the Incarnation and Resurrection. The Word of God is the measure by which all things were made. In light of the incarnation of the Word in the man Jesus, all human actions are capable of being an event in which God is known, made present. Every human being has unique and unrepeatable dignity. The love of neighbor fulfills the love of God. Human community is capable of transforming the world in the divine likeness. As Jesus taught, the last judgment will consist only in this, God's promise that "What you did to these least ones, you did to me." This Judeo-Christian ethic has shaped western thought and continues to fashion new moral perspectives on contemporary personal and social issues like capital punishment, war, human rights, and care of the poor and marginalized.

Faith and Science

The uniqueness of the Catholic Church is also expressed in its relationship to science. The Catholic Church encourages an ongoing dialogue between science and faith, not only among its scholars but among the faithful at large. Since the sixteenth century, Catholicism struggled in its encounter with science, originally fearing that scientific discoveries denied the revealed faith. Over the centuries the Catholic Church learned to use scientific knowledge in dialogue with faith. Both science and faith open the way to knowledge but of different things and in different ways. Science looks into the created world to discover its rules and functions. Faith looks at the world and human life to discover how it transcends itself, and faith searches for the One who is the measure of the world's transcendence. The dialogue between science and faith is central to questions like sharing of natural resources, population growth, birth control, abortion, transplants and cloning. This dialogue can be seen in the Church's acceptance of evolution as a means God used to develop life on earth. Catholic faith does not dispute evolution as science but insists that evolutionary theory alone cannot account for the relationship of the Creator with all creatures which is the foundation of the natural order. The dialogue with science continues in other areas.

The scientific question of homosexuality's origins has become a significant one for western cultures. On its resolution rest other questions of civil rights and even proposed changes in the definition of marriage. The Catholic Church has declared that persons who have homosexual tendencies must not be discriminated against. They have the right to membership in the Church and to serve in its ministries. The Church continues to follow the scientific research in this area but maintains that the question of the moral use of human sexuality must be determined by something in addition to science. Human sexuality is integral to human transcendence. Therefore, human sexuality must be used in a way that expresses faith in the One who created it, redeems it, and fulfills it by drawing human sexual expression between human partners into a transcendent relationship with God. Only sexual play and intercourse within a lifelong, monogamous and mutually faithful marriage between a man and a woman fully expresses the divine transcendence of which human sexual intercourse is capable.

Perhaps the least appreciated teaching of the Catholic Church is its stand on artificial birth control. The Catholic Church does not teach that parents must have all the children of which they are biologically capable. The Church's reasoning on birth control is that artificial means prevent the full sharing of life and the responsibility for life between a husband and wife that God designed marriage to be. Natural family planning, in contrast, deepens that sharing. Secondly, many of the means of artificial birth control do not prevent ovulation or fertilization but simply cause abortion by keeping a fertilized egg from implanting in the wall of the uterus. Among these means are birth control pills, hormonal injections, and an intrauterine device. Diaphragms and condoms are barriers to sperm. As such they are also barriers to the union of persons and to the completion of a natural sexual act. Their use implies a lack of sharing between spouses. Natural family planning helps to unify the spouses. Finally, the use of artificial birth control implies a judgment about the worth of human life. The child that may result without birth control is judged less desirable than the other things that the parents may obtain with the same resources they otherwise would use to rear the child. Natural family planning includes planning for the use of resources and the number of children a couple is able to rear according to their human and Christian dignity.

The Catholic Church's dialogue with science touches all areas but especially medical ethics. The Church acknowledges that every human person at each stage of development is called by God into a transcendent relationship. The Church, therefore, has developed a respect for human life in all its forms and at all its stages. While the Church encourages scientific research, it cautions that abortion, the cloning of humans and euthanasia are contrary to respect for human life. On the other hand, the Church encourages the gift of organ donation, as long as it does not exploit persons, as a way of sharing the gift of life with others. Nourishment and hydration for those who are impaired, and natural death assisted by pain relief are also important moral considerations in this dialogue.

World Religions and Cultures

The Catholic Church is not a monochrome structural uniformity but a multicultural interplay between faith and life. One poll of the Church's experience is of

God in Christ but the other is of the vast diversity of the earth and the human community into whose care it is given by God. The Church's life holds together the tension between the transcendence of God and the earthy, transitory nature of human experience and cultures. The Catholic Church developed by adapting to various cultures. In the process it also adopted practices from other world religions. Today, one of the great issues confronting the Church is how to continue to adapt to the rapidly changing cultural conditions in the ever shrinking global village.

In the period before the New Testament books were written, in the first decades of its life, the Catholic Church adapted the Jewish world view in which it was born to the Greek culture in which the faith was being preached and lived. The Church spread east among Jewish Christians whose descendants two millennia later still use Aramaic in their liturgy. The Church adapted in the first centuries to the culture in Lebanon and today the Maronite Church has its own unique forms and practices, customs and liturgy. Similarly, the Catholic faith adapted to Egyptian, Armenian, and Syrian cultures, as well as the cultures of Rome, and the northern European tribes. In each of these cultures, different liturgical, devotional and theological expressions created a truly Catholic or universal expression of Christian life.

The Catholic Church, in the first centuries and especially in the east, adapted customs that predate

Christianity. The use of incense in worship, sprinkling persons and articles with water as a sign of blessing, the use of icons and statues, oil lamps or candles, and the vestments of the clergy are all cultural adaptations that vary, depending on the area in which the Church lived when they were adopted. Music, chant, and prayer-forms are clearly cultural expressions which vary in the Church from location to location. Since the Second Vatican Council, the Church has been in a process of relearning how to adapt itself to diverse cultures, a charism it had severely restricted after Trent. This work of the Spirit holds great promise as the Church faces its next great cultural Everest, adapting the Catholic Faith to an increasingly secularized world-culture driven by materialist interests and projected into every part of the earth by mass communication.

7
Prayer

Prayer is a rhythm of life, the beat of the heart of God its meter. Some say that prayer raises the mind and heart to God, while others claim prayer is whatever God accepts. As clear or poetic as these definitions might be, in the end prayer is God at work in the person eliciting a response and effecting transformation into the divine likeness. Prayer begins with God's action and ends in union with God. Thus, prayer is a great mystery; those who pray are known by God and know God. Those who pray become one with God in some real way. The hearts of those who pray eventually beat with the rhythm of the heart of God and even become God. Prayer in Catholic life is divided into public or private forms and is analyzed by its traditional practices, such as reading God's word or speaking to God, listening to or seeking union with God. Private prayer is one heart speaking to another until both beat as one, and public prayer is God's heartbeat drawing a people into the rhythm of divine life which is mutual love. Both forms of prayer are synchronized within the liturgical cycle.

The Liturgical Year

The liturgical seasons permeate all time and all creation with the rhythm of the Church's prayer life that beats with the heart of God. The Greek word "liturgy" literally means public work; the Church's public work is the worship of God. That worship occurs in a rhythm that circles the calendar year. It breaks chronological time into sacred periods so that another kind of time, God's timing, can penetrate human affairs. *Chronos* is the Greek kind of time marked by calendars, clocks, appointments, births, and deaths. Another kind of time guides the liturgical year. *Kairos* is a bequest of eastern Christian tradition. *Kairos* permeates all chronologies and draws the events of time into the eternity of God. God's fulfillment happens as the minutes of chronological time slip by. The liturgical year breaks the circling calendar year into sacred events that allow God's timing to slip through the cracks in time. Charles Dickens described God's timing in *A Christmas Carol*. In one night, Christmas Eve, the spirits of Christmas past, present, and future converted the heart of Ebenezer Scrooge to the likeness of the Christ Child. Dickens' division of the spiritual power of Christmas Eve into past, present, and future reprised the Catholic liturgical season of Advent, the period of preparation for Christmas. In the sacred time of Advent's final hours, the spirits slipped into Scrooge's dark soul and worked their transformation.

Advent begins the Catholic liturgical year four Sundays prior to Christmas, celebrated on December 25. Christmas future, the Church's faith in Christ's second coming, rings in the first Sunday of Advent. The sacred liturgy repeats the ancient prayer from 1 Corinthians, Ch. 16, MARANATHA, "Come, Lord Jesus." It is the Church's response to Christ's promise to come again at the end of time. Should Christ not come "now," the Church continues to recall that God prepared the world for Christ's birth and the Church for his coming again in glory. The second and third Sundays of Advent recall Christmas past with readings from the prophets who announced the coming of Christ, especially John the Baptist, Christ's Forerunner. The final and fourth Sunday of Advent prepares the congregation for Christmas present by retelling over a three year cycle the Annunciation either to Joseph or to Mary, or through the proclamation of Elizabeth. The Roman Catholic liturgical calendar highlights a different synoptic Gospel (Matthew, Mark, or Luke) each year, beginning with the first Sunday of Advent. The Gospel passages chosen for the Christmas season are selected primarily from either Matthew or Luke, who each composed an infancy narrative. On Christmas Day the prologue of the Gospel according to John is proclaimed, announcing that the incarnate Word not only dwells with humankind but offers to those who receive him the power to become the daughters and sons of God.

The Christmas season begins on Christmas Eve and continues through the celebration of Epiphany, which recalls the visit to Bethlehem of astrologers seeking the newborn King of the Jews. The Baptism of the Lord signals the beginning of Christ's public ministry to mark him as the Beloved Son. According to ancient practice in the Roman Church, Epiphany is celebrated January 6 (the traditional twelfth day of Christmas) and the Baptism of the Lord on January 13. In the United States, these celebrations are transferred to the nearest Sunday. The eighth day of Christmas, January first, was called the Feast of the Circumcision and later the Holy Name of Jesus. Now it is kept as the celebration of Mary as the Mother of God. It honors Mary as the mother of Jesus, who is God and man in one person without confusion or mixing of natures. In the eastern Catholic tradition, emphasis is placed not on his birth but on three manifestations of Christ to the nations as God, Redeemer, and Lord. The coming of the magi reveals Christ to peoples beyond Israel, the Baptism of the Lord attests he is Beloved Son of the Father, and Christ's first miracle at Cana in Galilee where he changed water into wine, manifests his divine power. Epiphany itself means manifestation and these three events comprise Christ's initial manifestation as the one sent by God to fulfill the ancient promises made to Israel.

The celebration of the first six weeks of the liturgical calendar illustrates that the entire liturgical year is an extended meditation on the Word of God. The Church yearns to listen again and again to the Word of God and enflesh the good news in its life. Through the Church's public prayer or liturgy, there is a continuous proclamation of the sacred scriptures. The reason is simple. A long Catholic tradition believes that the Word of God is living and active. What it declares is made truly present in the liturgy for the sake of those who believe. Consequently, the liturgical year is not a simple annual recall of past events in the salvation of humankind but a vibrant and present invitation to share in the saving power of God. This invitation to share in salvation is particularly evident in the seasons of Lent and Easter, the pivotal core of the liturgical cycle.

Lent is a preparation of 40 days for the 50 days or seven weeks of Easter celebration. Forty is a biblical number signifying an indeterminate period of time for conversion. The Hebrews traversed the desert for 40 years before they were prepared to enter the Promised Land. Christ was led into the desert by the Spirit of God imparted at his baptism. Through 40 days of fasting, prayer, and finally of temptation he was prepared for his earthly ministry. Christ's ministry of salvation culminated in his death and resurrection, his Passover or Pasch. Lent prepares the Christian to enter by baptism into Christ's death and resurrection, the Paschal mystery. The seven weeks of Easter celebrate that

Paschal mystery's power to transform the world. Seven is another mystical, biblical number which indicates the perfection of all time or the divine completion of time. Resurrection from the dead which was promised for the end of time has already begun. Christ is the first-born of many brothers and sisters who will rise at the end of time. Eternity shattered time with the resurrection of Christ. Both Lent and Pasch are derived from words to signal springtime. This part of the liturgical year is constituted as both a celebration and enactment of God's recreation of the world. God's Kairos becomes a kind of springtime. This springtime is introduced by the readings of the first two Sundays of Lent. The first Sunday's Gospel passage recalls the temptation of Christ in the desert and the second Sunday his transfiguration. These liturgies present Christ suffering our temptations in his humanity and at the same time being God's testimony to our transformation in his likeness. Christ's Passover in Jerusalem effects in our humanity the revelation of his divine glory. Lent opens with a liturgical proclamation of the eternal plan of God. We are to share in Christ's divinity, who humbled himself to share in our humanity. This penitential season initiates a hope-filled message. Nothing will frustrate the plan of God, who desires to complete our humanity through the death and resurrection of Christ.

Easter, according to ancient tradition, is celebrated in the western Catholic Church on the first Sunday after the first full moon following the vernal or spring equinox. The interplay between Chronos and Kairos is clearly the energy that rotates the liturgical cycle. The setting of the date for Easter in turn determines other celebrations in the cycle. Lent begins on Ash Wednesday, six Sundays and four days prior to Easter. The four days were added in the distant past when it became important to be accurate about an exact 40 days of fasting. Each Sunday of the year is a little Easter and one does not fast at Easter. This left only 36 days for fasting in the six weeks of Lent and required the addition of four extra days, which made a Wednesday the beginning of Lent. Ashes are the burned palm branches retained from the previous year's celebration of the Sunday of the Lord's Passion, nicknamed Palm Sunday. That is the only Sunday of the liturgical year on which the entire account of the Lord's passion and death is publicly read from one of the synoptic gospels. Passion Sunday begins the week called Holy at the end of which three sacred days mark the transition into the Easter Season. These are the Easter Triduum.

The Triduum begins with a celebration of the Eucharist during which the feet of at least some of the congregation are washed. This commemoration of the last supper during which Jesus washed the feet of his disciples occurs on the evening of Thursday of Holy Week. In the early centuries of the Christian era, this was the night public sinners were reconciled to the Christian assembly, so that the baptized who had fallen away from the life of Christ through serious sin, such as adultery, murder, or apostasy, might be reunited with the assembly and be ready to receive the catechumens who had spent Lent preparing for baptism. Holy Thursday is sometimes called Maundy Thursday, from the commandment or mandatum of Christ given according to John at the last supper, "love one another as I have loved you." The Triduum continues on Good Friday with the solemn reading of the passion of Christ according to John, the veneration of a wooden cross, and the reception of communion reserved from the previous evening's Eucharist. Those familiar with the Passover accounts will recall that the Hebrews were permitted to eat of the Paschal lamb the day after the angel of death had passed over their homes. Otherwise, the Eucharist is not celebrated from Holy Thursday night until after dark on Holy Saturday when the first Mass of Easter is offered at the Easter Vigil.

Catholic liturgical observance reflects an ancient Hebrew designation of the day beginning with sunset and the oncoming of darkness. According to Genesis, God created light and separated the light from the darkness and there was "evening and morning the first day." Easter begins as does Christmas in the darkness of the night after sunset. That is also why Catholics can celebrate an anticipatory or vigil Eucharist every Sunday of the year on Saturday evening. Sunday celebrations may begin all year long as early as 4 p.m., the time of winter darkness in upper latitudes. However, on Holy Saturday we must truly wait until after nightfall to begin the

Easter Vigil. This great vigil expresses the Church's faith that Easter celebrates a new creation in which the resurrection of Jesus permeates all time, overcomes all darkness, and draws creation into the divine transformation promised by God at its making, into resurrection and eternal light.

Other events recorded in the New Testament about the resurrection of Jesus also have a place in the seven weeks of Easter celebration. The Sunday after Easter Sunday is now called Mercy Sunday. The Gospel passage on this day from John proclaims the power given the disciples by the risen Christ to forgive sins and recalls how the doubt of Thomas was transformed into the Christian creed that Jesus is both Lord and God. According to the Acts of the Apostles, the ascension of Jesus into heaven took place 40 days after his resurrection, and so the celebration of the Ascension of the Lord is set on a Thursday, an actual 40 days after Easter Sunday. The last day of the Easter season is called Pentecost Sunday, which means the 50th day. Pentecost, a Jewish feast celebrated fifty days after the Passover, is the day Acts indicates that the Spirit of God came upon the disciples, beginning the Church's mission to prepare the world for Christ's coming again at the end of time.

The periods between Christmas and Lent and from Pentecost to the beginning of a new liturgical year are named Ordinary Time, from ordinal or counted. During ordinary time the Church celebrates other events in the life of Christ and of his disciples, particularly Mary his mother and the other saints. The entire calendar year is sanctified by commemorating God's great work in Christ and in the lives of his disciples. Among the biblical commemorations is the Transfiguration of the Lord, celebrated on August 6, forty days before the Triumph of the Cross on September 14. The later feast honors an archeological event, the discovery almost three centuries after Christ's death of the cross on which he died. Helena, the mother of the Emperor Constantine, is credited with discovering the cross in Jerusalem. Another biblical event in the life of Christ is the Presentation of the Lord in the Temple, celebrated on February 2, 40 days after his birth. Luke indicates that this was the period prescribed to elapse for the purification of Mary according to the Mosaic Law.

The commemoration of saints includes many of those mentioned in the New Testament as well as those whose lives inspired Christians in subsequent eras. Among these festivals is the birth of John the Baptist. It is celebrated on June 24, just after the summer solstice, as darkness begins to increase in the northern hemisphere, and recalls John's prophecy, "He [Christ] must increase, and I must decrease." The traditional celebration of Christ's birth that heralds God's enlightening the world follows the other solar solstice and coincides with the return of the sun in the winter. The birth of Mary, September 8, follows nine months after her immaculate conception, December 8. According to Catholic faith, her immaculate conception prepared

Mary to be the sinless mother of God's Son. There are memorials of one or more of the Twelve Apostles, St. Paul, and the Evangelists scattered over the twelve calendar months. Other saints, holy men, women, and even children are usually remembered on the day of their death or burial — for instance, Francis of Assisi on his death date, October 4, or Thomas More, the man for all seasons, on June 22. Mary of Magdala is commemorated July 22 and Martha of Bethany, who welcomed Jesus as a guest in her home, on July 29. The Holy Innocents, children murdered in Bethlehem by Herod's order, are recalled December 28 within the Christmas season, as is Stephen the first martyr on December 26. It was on Stephen's feast that the medieval carol tells us good King Wenseslaus, himself a revered saint of Bohemia, looked out to see a poor man gathering winter fuel and went to share with him the bounty of Christmas. St. Wenseslaus who was martyred by his brother's henchmen is remembered on September 28. Even Angels have their feast days, Michael, Gabriel and Raphael on September 29, and the Holy Guardian Angels on October 2.

The many festivals, memorials and feasts that occur in liturgical Ordinary Time repeat the rhythm of the Paschal mystery of Easter in the life of the Church. God is at work in the faithful, moving the People of God to empty themselves by martyrdom, ministry, and especially charity for the sake of God's eternal gift of unitive love, the Kingdom of Heaven. Historically it is no small wonder that within the ordinary things of the human enterprise the liturgical cycles have generated so much art and architecture, story and song, literature and poetry. The Sabbaths and other days of rest, refreshment, and human fellowship complete this recurring reflection on the divine revelation. In Catholic life the liturgical cycle testifies that all times and seasons, indeed all creation, responds by the power of the Holy Spirit to the saving work of God in Christ.

Public Prayer - The Liturgy

The public work of the Church is the worship of God through which the Church shares the divine life. Public worship, called the Divine Liturgy, includes the celebration of the sacraments of the Church and the Liturgy of the Hours. Celebration of the sacraments sanctifies the lives of the faithful. The Liturgy of the Hours sanctifies the day by using various psalms and Biblical canticles and marking seven periods of prayer.

The source and summit of the liturgical life of the Catholic Church is the Liturgy of the Eucharist. This liturgy is best known among Roman Catholics by its nickname, in Latin Missa, in English the Mass. "Ite, Missa est." was the dismissal at the end of the Latin liturgy. Some think the best translation of this Latinism is, "Go, the mission awaits." The Mass is the great commission, Christ sending his disciples into the world for its salvation. They have heard God's Word in the liturgy and become one with the sacrifice of Christ through which they offer themselves to God. The People of God are now sent, commissioned to be themselves the living Eugharist in the midst of the world for its transformation in communion with God. Catholic moral theology and social teaching flows from the Eucharist and finds its fulfillment in it. By coming more and more into communion with Christ whose body and blood they have shared in the Eucharist, the faithful are agents of God's mercy in the world and are to bring the world to communion with the Merciful One. The public work of the Church animated by the Holy Spirit is to bring all creation to God in Christ, so that God may be all in all. As such, all the works of the Church begin with and find their completion in the Eucharist, the foretaste of the eternal banquet in the Kingdom.

The Liturgy of the Eucharist - Introduction

The word Eucharist, from the Greek for thanksgiving, is used in several different ways. The Eucharist can denote the sacrament of the Body and Blood of Christ which the faithful receive in the form of bread and wine. It also is used for the reception of that sacrament, as in "to receive the Eucharist." In both instances, Eucharist is interchangeable with the term "Holy Communion." The Liturgy of the Eucharist is a sacramental participation in the sacrifice Christ offered of himself to the Father and of his disciples with himself as an acceptable gift to God. This liturgy is celebrated in two parts, the Liturgy of the Word, which culminates in the proclamation of the Gospel, and the Liturgy of the Eucharist, whose centerpiece is the Eucharistic Prayer proclaimed over the bread, the wine, and the people by a bishop or priest/presbyter. In the Latin Church, the Mass is a very plastic ritual which can unfold over a period of two hours or more on special occasions or as little as twenty minutes on weekday mornings in most parishes. In the eastern rites of the Church, the Eucharist is called the Divine Liturgy and is less plastic, particularly formalized in its celebration, of a pronounced mystical character, and more consistently of greater length.

A rite is a prescribed action that carries a certain meaning. When capitalized, Rite means an entire set of standards for the community's life and worship and is used with the proper name of the observant community or communities, as in the Byzantine Rite or the Oriental Rites. In the Roman Rite, there are multiple entrance rites, from which the presider may choose, and a concluding rite. The several entrance rites that begin the Mass are designed to focus the congregation's attention on God's presence so that they may fully and consciously participate in the worship of God. The entrance rites include a psalm passage or hymn, followed by a sign of the cross using the Trinitarian formula also used at baptism, "In the name of the Father, and of the Son and of the Holy Spirit." The presider then greets the assembly in the name of God, "The Lord be with you," and follows with a penitential rite asking forgiveness of sins. On Sundays, a rite of sprinkling may replace the penitential rite. Sprinkling the assembly with blessed water recalls their baptism into Christ's death and resurrection by which they gained admittance to the Eucharistic assembly. The Glory to God is sung next on Sundays and great feasts. It is an ancient hymn praising the Holy Trinity. A prayer offered by the presider, who is either a bishop or a priest, concludes the entrance rites. After the Liturgy of the Eucharist, the liturgy concludes with announcements about the life and work of the congregation, a blessing in the name of the Holy Trinity, and a dismissal, such as, "Go in Peace, to love and serve the Lord."

Mass - The Liturgy of the Word

Readings for the Liturgy of the Word are taken from a lectionary. The formulation of the Roman Catholic lectionary is the product of several centuries. A large portion of the Bible is divided into selections for use on Sundays and various memorials. Since Vatican II, the lectionary has been revised through consultation involving bishops, biblical and liturgical experts, and final approval by the Pope. The first reading at Mass on most Sundays of the year is from the Old Testament. It sets the background for the Gospel passage read later in the liturgy and expresses the Church's faith that the Law and the Prophets testify to Christ. Then a psalm meditation on the meaning of the

Old Testament passage is sung or recited. The psalms also testify to Christ according to the faith of his earliest Jewish followers. Peter quotes the second psalm, in his Pentecost sermon in the Acts of the Apostles, as a prophecy of the resurrection of Jesus. After the psalm, a selection from one of the letters of the Apostles is read. This selection is tied loosely to the Gospel of the day and during Ordinary Time is a continuous reading from the chosen letter over succeeding Sundays.

Finally, the assembly, seated since the conclusion of the entrance rites, rises to greet the Risen Christ who speaks to them through the Gospel. As the congregation rises, all sing Alleluia, the ancient Hebrew word meaning "Praise God." The Church praises God's work of salvation manifest in the Risen Lord. The Gospel is then proclaimed by a deacon or a priest who makes the sign of the cross over the book and on his forehead, lips, and over his heart. Those assembled repeat this signing of the senses. This ritual signing with the cross focuses the attention of the listener on Christ, who opens the scriptures and explains his saving work. A homily follows the proclamation of the Gospel. An ordained minister reflects on the readings and their meaning for Christian living. On Sundays after the homily, the congregation stands and declares the faith of the whole Church using the Nicene Creed that dates from 324 A.D. The Liturgy of the Word concludes with general intercessions for the needs of the universal Church, the assembled faithful, the world, and the faithful departed.

Mass - The Liturgy of the Eucharist

The Liturgy of the Eucharist enacts the Gospel proclaimed at the Mass. Bread and wine are brought forward, as well as donations from the assembly for the work of the Church. A small amount of water is mixed with the wine as the deacon or priest prays, "By the mystery of this wine and water may we come to share in the divinity of Christ who humbled himself to share in our humanity." Praise of God is offered for the gifts and all are invited to pray that God will find the sacrifice to be offered a pleasing gift. This gift is not simply bread and wine but also the assembly who join themselves through the Eucharistic prayer to Christ and his sacrifice once offered on the cross. Catholics understand that neither the presider nor the assembly worship by their own effort alone. Liturgy is God's work in them and among them. This is why Catholic Christians believe that the Liturgy of the Eucharist, and indeed every liturgy, is the work of the Holy Spirit. The Spirit is the one who drew from the Virgin Mary the body and human life of the Word Incarnate. The same Spirit is the power by which God raised Jesus from the dead. The Word of God heard at Mass is inspired in its writing and in its proclamation by the Spirit who is also at work in the one who hears and believes. By the invocation of that same Spirit, both the gifts of bread and wine and those who offer them are made holy and become the body and blood of Christ. This invocation is made by the presiding bishop or priest in the Eucharistic Prayer. The presider also speaks over the elements the words of Jesus at the Last Supper, "This is my Body... This is my Blood..." The congregation gives assent to this prayer with their "Amen." Their assent expresses the Church's faith that through the liturgy the faithful partake in the Trinitarian life. The Spirit makes them a pleasing gift to God with Christ. This is the meaning of the doxology that concludes the Eucharistic Prayer: "Through him, with him, and in him, in the unity of the Holy Spirit, all glory and honor are yours, Almighty Father, for ever and ever. AMEN."

The rite of receiving communion follows the Eucharistic Prayer. First the assembly prays together the prayer Jesus taught his disciples, the Our Father. Next, all are invited to share a sign of peace in Christ. Then, accompanied by a litany to the Lamb of God, the presider breaks the Eucharistic bread so all may know the presence of the risen Lord whom they receive as one. As the assembly receives communion, they feed on their own likeness, the Spirit having transformed them and the gifts they receive into Christ. Communion is offered under one or both of its forms, bread and wine. It is Catholic faith that the whole Christ, body and blood, soul of his humanity, and eternal divinity, are received in either or both forms. For many centuries the presider alone received both the Eucharistic bread and the cup of the Lord's blood. Everyone else received only in the form of bread. Since the Second Vatican Council in the 1960s, the Church returned to a more ancient practice and it is common once again for all to drink from the cup.

The Seven Sacraments

The pattern for the Mass is found as early as Luke's resurrection account on the road to Emmaus. The regular Sunday celebration by the first disciples of the Liturgy of the Eucharist possibly inspired the diptych form of the narrative with its liturgy of Word and of Eucharist. The liturgy of the Word unfolds on the first day of the week, the day the Church celebrates his resurrection, as Christ opens the meaning of the Jewish scriptures for two downcast disciples. As they make their way home from Jerusalem after his passion, Jesus, though unrecognized, joins their company and in response to their dismay explains why the Messiah had to suffer so as to enter into his glory. When they arrive at their home, he accepts their invitation to dinner. During the meal in a ritual breaking of the bread, he makes himself known and they recognize the Risen Lord. A century after Luke composed that narrative, a Christian convert at Rome, Justin (162 A.D.), wrote an explanation of the beliefs and practices of the Catholic faith. His description of the Sunday celebration of the Mass shows in every detail the structure of the present Sunday Liturgy of the Eucharist in a Catholic parish. Justin also described the prerequisites for participation in the Eucharist, specifically the sacraments of Baptism and Chrismation, better known among Roman Catholics as Confirmation.

Baptism and Chrismation are two of the seven sacraments celebrated in the Catholic Liturgy. A sacrament is a way to encounter God in creation. Christ Jesus is in his humanity the great sacrament of the encounter with God. The Church is the sacrament or fullest encounter with Christ in this creation. The seven sacraments are the Church's ritual practices, in which a person comes to share in a unique way in the life of God offered to the world in Christ. This share is given by the Spirit through the prayer of the Church enacted in these ritual actions or signs. For instance, in Baptism water is poured as the name of the Holy Trinity is pronounced over the person. "Baptize" means in Greek "to go down into." The words of Catholic Baptism are, "I baptize you in the name of the Father, and the Son, and the Holy Spirit." The action of pouring the water with these words made effective by the Spirit is a sign of immersion into the life of the Trinity, revealed through the death and resurrection of Jesus. In baptism, the person dies with Christ to sin and death and rises with him to the new life of God, an eternal enduring love. All Catholic sacraments are prayer/actions that effect through the working of the Holy Spirit the reality that their symbols, like the pouring of water, anointing with oil, or eating bread and wine, signify.

The liturgical celebration of Baptism and indeed all the sacraments of the Church flow toward the

Eucharist and find their fulfillment there. Three of the seven sacraments initiate persons into the Church, itself the Body of Christ in the midst of the world. These are Baptism, Confirmation, and Eucharist. The Church considers Baptism so necessary for salvation for someone who believes in Christ that even a non-believer may in necessity baptize a person who has faith in Christ. Chrismation or Confirmation completes baptism, sealing the baptized with God's Spirit and more fully conforming the Christian to the likeness of Christ sent by the Father into the world for its salvation. Chrismation is given by a bishop or priest who lays his hands upon the head of the one to be confirmed and anoints the person with perfumed oil consecrated by a bishop. This consecrated oil, Sacred Chrism, is the outward sign of the inner flowing of the Spirit, the gift of the Father. Baptism and Confirmation admit the initiate to the Eucharist. The Eucharist completes initiation into the Body of Christ. Sunday celebrations of the Eucharist deepen and expand participation in the life of the Holy Trinity, who animates the communion of the Church.

In Catholic practice both adults and children receive all three sacraments of initiation in a single celebration of initiation. Baptizing and Chrismating infants, and in some cases giving the Eucharist, is the practice of the eastern churches throughout the centuries. Roman Catholics baptize infants but delay Confirmation until later in life. Roman Catholic practice with regard to receiving First Communion was to delay admitting a child until after Confirmation. Exceptions were made in danger of death. In the early twentieth century, Pope St. Pius X allowed children baptized as infants and catechized as young children to receive communion around the age of seven years even though not yet confirmed. This practice is still usual in many countries. The revised Code of Canon Law (1983) specifies that an unbaptized person eight years or older must be catechized and initiated through the ancient triple sacramental rites given in one liturgical celebration.

Two of the sacraments heal or restore the life of Christ in the baptized who have sinned. These are Penance and the Anointing of the Sick. The rites celebrating both sacraments include the laying on of hands by a bishop or priest. This action, as in Confirmation, confers the Spirit of God and denotes the giving in Confirmation, or restoring in Penance and Anointing, of the person's place at the altar, the Lord's Table. The sacrament of Penance, better known as confession, is celebrated in the Rite of Reconciliation. This rite reconciles persons who through grave sin have rejected the life of Christ given in baptism and prepares them once again to share in the Eucharistic assembly. The sacrament of Penance enacts the mandate of Christ, found in the Gospel according to John, "Receive the Holy Spirit. Whose sins you forgive are forgiven..." Historical development of the ritual for Penance is long and complex. Today the rite may be celebrated one of three ways: in a communal setting with a small congregation and including a full liturgy of the Word, in a private setting with only a single penitent and priest, or less frequently as general absolution of a large number of persons who are in some extreme situation and cannot individually confess their sins to a priest.

In his New Testament letter the Apostle James tells Christians to call for the presbyters to anoint the sick among them and pray for them. The Lord will restore the sick to health and forgive their sins through this anointing and prayer made in faith. This anointing of the sick was known for centuries as Extreme Unction or Last Anointing, implying preparation for death. Historically illnesses were more often fatal than they are today in developed nations. Illness also is often the occasion for conversion, recognition of sinful offenses, and the desire to receive forgiveness and make amends. The Church seeks in anointing the Christian to strengthen the gifts of faith, hope, and love that sustain the Christian life and bring real healing to the spirit of the person. This spiritual healing has its corollary healing in the mind and body. Today, the Church anoints the chronically ill, those preparing for surgery, the elderly who are burdened by their years, as well as those who are in danger of death. While Anointing of the Sick is part of the last rites for a Catholic in preparation for death, the last sacrament to be received is the Eucharist. The last rite of the Church is the last reception of the Eucharist called in Latin *Viaticum*, literally meaning "to take with you along the way." In this last reception of the Eucharist the Church recalls the twenty-third psalm and the Good Shepherd who spreads a banquet for the person who walks in the shadow of death.

The last two of the seven sacraments strengthen persons to respond to the call of God with their whole lives, thus enriching the Church with family life and with ordained ministries. These are Matrimony and Holy Orders, the sacraments of vocation or calling. Each of these sacraments has a well developed and complex history, theology, and set of Church laws defining it.

The Catholic Church has been formulating laws concerning entrance into marriage since the time of St. Paul, who told Christians at Corinth that one could enter a second marriage if a pagan partner would not allow a person to live as a Christian. Before there were nation states in Europe, the Church had well developed laws concerning marriage. These laws influenced subsequent civil legislation on marriage in western countries. In Church law, marriage is a natural right which when entered by two baptized persons becomes a sacramental way of life. Since the Church recognizes it as a natural reality, marriage's definition corresponds first to nature. In the natural order of things, two persons come together to form a lasting bond that benefits the human community by their life-long care of each other and through their giving birth to and educating children for the welfare of their society. This natural bond of marriage most clearly and fundamentally occurs in the joining of a man and a woman. That marriage should be monogamous is reasonable, since it is the experience of many cultures and the Church's reflection on the Scriptures that the dignity of both men and women is better supported by monogamy than by polygamy or polyandry.

The mutual consent of a man and a woman to a life-long, exclusive and faithful partnership constitutes the covenant of marriage in Roman Catholic tradition. Consent in normal circumstances must be expressed before a minister of the Church and two witnesses. Catholics believe every baptized person is in a real way the presence of Christ in the world. The marriage of two baptized persons is more than a natural reality; they share Christ with each other as they share themselves with each other. They are sacraments, means of sharing the life of God one with the other. Their children too share this life by their birth into a domestic church, and first come to know Christ in the lives of their parents. Sacramental marriage is not only a natural right for a man and a woman but also the fundamental unit of human society. It is in the Church the most fundamental manifestation of the communion of persons, mirroring the Church's share in the life of Christ. Catholics are obliged by Church law to marry another Catholic so that they may be assured of living a sacramental life. Bishops regularly dispense Catholics from this obligation if they desire to marry a baptized Christian who is not in communion with the Church, or even someone who is not baptized. The law exists to emphasize the faith of the Church, not to impede the natural right of any person to choose a marriage partner. Still, marriage is a way of life to which a person is called by God, a vocation. Its nature as a sacrament is most clearly recognized when the spouses rely not upon themselves alone but upon the Lord who strengthens them. Catholic marriages are nurtured at the Eucharist and family life strengthened by introducing children to the Gospel and a share in the Trinitarian life through the sacraments of the Church.

Ordination is the Church's public affirmation of a call from God experienced by the candidate and subsequently submitted to the bishop and the whole Church for confirmation as being truly God's will. Requesting ordination is a personal response to God's invitation to minister to God's People and to grow in holiness. A person called by God is given a new place at the Eucharistic table through the sacrament of Holy Orders. The place given at the Eucharistic table is appropriate to the overall ministry that the newly ordained will live out in the Church. There are three orders or places into which a person may be ordained — deacon, presbyter, or bishop.

The deacon stands at the table in service of the bishop and the assembly, proclaiming the Gospel and the General Intercessions, assisting with the preparation of the gifts of bread and wine, and giving to the faithful the cup of the Lord's Blood. The ministry of the deacon in the Church is to proclaim the Word of God by serving the various practical needs of the People of God, especially the poor. The presbyters form a college or assembly around the bishop called the Presbyterate. The common title for a presbyter is priest, a name originally used only for the bishop. The priests represent the bishop when he cannot be present to celebrate the Eucharist, which occurs regularly because of the number of parishes and liturgies needed to accommodate the faithful for whom the bishop is responsible as chief pastor. Presbyters surround the bishop at Mass sharing in the Eucharistic Prayer and offering communion to the faithful. In the absence of the Bishop, they are the presiders at the Eucharistic Liturgy and pastors of congregations, and so they have the ministries of the pastoral care of the faithful, preaching, teaching, presiding at the celebration of sacraments, and the administration of church affairs in local parishes.

A bishop is a successor of the Apostles who were sent, as the name in Greek (apostolos) implies, to be ambassadors, or vicars, for Christ. The Bishop of a diocese is the Vicar of Christ who is the Head of his Body, the Church. The bishop represents Christ the Head in the assembly of the faithful gathered to celebrate the Liturgy. As the Vicar of Christ, the bishop presides at the Liturgy of the Eucharist. For this reason the Church's official teaching is only men can be ordained as bishops and presbyters. Human sexuality is an integral dimension of personhood. Those who preside in the person of Christ, as Head of his Body, must be male since Christ's incarnation as Head of his Body is in the masculine gender. Only the bishop may ordain persons to the deaconate and priesthood or with other bishops ordain someone to the order of bishop. Ordination occurs through the laying on of hands and an extended prayer particular to the order being conferred. In this way the bishop assigns the person to a new place around the Eucharistic table and thus to new ministries for the sake of the whole Church.

The Liturgy of the Hours

The Liturgy of the Hours is an ancient form of public prayer. Also called the Divine Office, this liturgy occupies a person or community in sanctifying the hours of each day through the praise of God. The origin of the Hours is the Jewish practice of praying the psalms and canticles of the Bible at various times throughout the day. The Hours have developed over the entire twenty centuries of Christian prayer. Today they take a variety of forms, some brief and others more complex. The primary influences in its development are reflected in the names given these forms, such as the cathedral office which is simplified for use with a congregation, or the monastic office which has a longer form. The Liturgy of the Hours is the principal occupation of monks and cloistered nuns, but the laity also are encouraged to participate in the principal Hours of the office whether in groups, especially in their parish churches, or individually. All ordained persons take on the obligation to pray the Liturgy of the Hours daily.

The Hours were established before the modern clock was invented. They describe seven periods of prayer. The principal Hours are morning and evening prayer, whose ancient names were Lauds, meaning Praise, and Vespers. It is the custom to sing some or all of the psalms and canticles, at least during the principal hours. At morning and evening prayer a canticle from the Gospel according to Luke is included. The canticle sung by John the Baptist's father, Zachariah, at the birth of his son marks the morning praises and the canticle of Mary, the Mother of God, is the evening lullaby. There are three little moments or Hours of prayer between morning and evening. A simple night prayer is offered before sleep. It includes the canticle of Simeon, who received the Christ child into his arms in the Temple and declared that having seen this Light of God he could rest in eternal peace. The Hour of Readings or Matins is the seventh hour of prayer that sanctifies the day. It is usually celebrated in monasteries in the darkness before dawn. According to the psalms, the Word of God is a lamp for the believer, showing the way to the Lord. This office of readings is used to begin the Easter Vigil and prepares the candidates for the sacraments of initiation. The daily office of readings includes the writings of various saints, mystics, and theologians along with psalms and scriptures.

Few of the laity pray the Hours and most are unaware of the existence of this heritage of Catholic liturgical prayer. If known at all, it is presumed to be reserved for the religious and clergy. This is particularly evident in places where the Hours could be the center of life and prayer for parishes without priests to celebrate the Eucharist. Little, however, has been done to engage the laity in this liturgical form, itself developed by lay religious men and women, the first monks and nuns. Instead, the laity have used a wealth of diverse private prayer practices to compensate for a dearth of interest in the Liturgy of the Hours.

Private Prayer and Devotions

The Divine Word, the pattern for creation, is addressed through creation to the human heart and can be known to all. Unable by God's creative design to complete itself, creation is nonetheless open to revealing the pattern of the Word by which it was made and through which it is to be fulfilled. In Catholic life all things are capable of being prayer because of the radical value of creation that has been revealed by the Incarnation of God's Word. The opening of creation to reveal the Word is accomplished by the Spirit of God. Thus by Word and Spirit all things pray to God and through prayer seek their fullness in God. In the Catholic Tradition lighting a candle, sprinkling water, walking or kneeling, looking at an icon or statue, or holding something or someone can be prayer.

There are far too many prayer forms to mention here, but they all have a common root in *Lectio Divina*, the practice of *reading* the Word of God, meditating and responding to the Word, and contemplating God. Reading for centuries meant speaking the words of the book, not silently thinking them. The words had weight and taste and were meant to be heard and savored, repeated and ingested, until the person became the carrier of the Word of God. This kind of "reading" led to meditation. Meditation is close reading, attention to the details, to the feel, to the very presence of the event that one is "reading." In meditation, "reading" becomes being there and being a part of the mystery that is unfolding by the Spirit's power. It would not be unusual then to pass to the next dimension of *Lectio* which is to speak. *Oratio* is the verbal prayer that arises as one responds to the event, to the mystery. Having "heard" in meditation a fully embodied experience of the Word, one is moved by the Spirit to respond, to speak about the things that arise in one's heart and mind. However, because one is responding to the Divine Mystery, and not just to words, this *Oratio* ultimately is never enough. If one stays with prayer, one will be carried to the dimension called contemplation, so that the response of prayer may match God's intimacy with the person. Contemplation is becoming silent, as God is the silence that speaks. Contemplation happens through non-productive presence to God whose presence cannot be grasped but grasps the one who prays. These movements, from reading to meditation, from prayer to contemplation and back again to reading, occur in all the private prayer forms and devotions of the Church.

Two of the most familiar Catholic devotions are the Stations of the Cross and the Rosary. Both follow the form of *Lectio Divina*. Both became popular in the Middle Ages after pilgrimage to Jerusalem became an unavailable form of prayer. The Stations of the Cross allowed the Christian to walk in the footsteps of Jesus as he went to his passion. The Stations are usually prayed by walking to fourteen locations that recall events in the passion of Christ. The number and title of the Stations has varied over the centuries, and Pope John Paul II offered a modern change in the sequence. The events that are presented at each station or stopping place are drawn from the Gospel accounts of Christ's journey to Calvary. Some of the stations are literally events in his passing, while others are meditations on its overall meaning. An example of meditation on the overall meaning is the station known as "Veronica's Veil." The Greek name "Veronica" means "True Image." The station is a *midrash*, a Jewish way of giving the reader the meaning of the text by telling a story about it. The text is of course the passion of Christ, but the story told is of a woman who seeing him in the midst of his passion goes to him from out of the crowd of bystanders and comforts him by wiping his sweating and blood spattered face with her veil. As the story goes, when she returned home and removed her veil, she saw there imprinted the likeness of his face. Of course, the story is ultimately a question, "When have you seen him and comforted him?" Those who can answer that question have seen his true image and cared for him in their suffering neighbor. The Stations of the Cross mean to place the devotee at the events of the Passion, to gain intimate knowledge of Christ's suffering and come away changed. Such conversion is not simply the result of personal effort but relies on Word and Spirit to accomplish it in the person who prays.

A rosary was used in many religions before it became a Catholic practice. Taoism, Hinduism and Buddhism all use rosaries. Eastern Catholics use a rosary to pray the ancient Jesus Prayer, "Lord Jesus Christ, Son of the Living God, have mercy on me a sinner." The Roman Catholic rosary is a meditation on the biblical events of Christ's birth, ministry, death, and resurrection. These events are the great mysteries of our redemption accomplished through Jesus, a man like us. The Rosary draws one into the contemplation of these mysteries so that the Spirit may transform the one who prays into Christ's likeness as Son of God. The problem of course is that most people think that a rosary is a set of beads. In fact a rosary as a religious article is really a timepiece. Before ever a person is given this timer, she should read or hear the biblical testimony concerning Christ. Luke is especially good at narrating the events in the early life of the Lord. Once one has memorized the biblical events, for instance the

Annunciation, the Visitation, the Birth at Bethlehem, the Presentation in the Temple, and the Finding of the Boy Jesus in the Temple, one is ready to meditate on these mysteries in which God is revealed. At that point a timer can be handy, so that one may know how long to meditate on each event. Meditate as long as it takes to pray a brief prayer called the "Hail Mary" ten times for each mystery. Each decade of beads is a reflection on one of the biblical events. The "Hail Mary" is itself a scriptural prayer combining the words of the Angel Gabriel greeting Mary at Nazareth with the words of Elizabeth whom Mary subsequently visited. To these biblical phrases are added an *Oratio*, a spoken prayer that she who conceived the Word by the power of the Spirit will pray for us now and at the hour of our death. One may wonder why Catholics add such prayers to Mary to the scriptural verses. That is the topic of the next chapter, the Communion of Saints.

8
The Communion of Saints

God is Holy. To share the life of God is to be holy as God is Holy. Holiness is a divine gift given to the saints. The Latin term for holy is *sanctus* from which the English term "saint" is derived. All of Catholic life is a share in the holiness of God; its purpose, to bring that divine likeness to completion in heaven. As Athanasius put it, "God became man so that man could become God." Sainthood is identity with God in Christ. What is his is also the saint's. All the members of the Church are called to holiness of life now and likeness to God in the world to come (I John 3:1-3). All are called to be saints.

On Earth as in Heaven

In Isaiah 6:3, the prophet hears the cry of the Seraphim who worship before the throne of God in heaven: "Holy, Holy, Holy is the Lord of hosts!" This shout is incorporated into the Church's earthly liturgy as a response to the beginning of the Eucharistic Prayer, echoing on earth the worship given God by all the saints in heaven. Catholic liturgical inclusion of the saints is canonized in Revelations, the last book of the New Testament. A vision of the heavenly liturgy is given on a Sunday to the author by Jesus who is dressed as the High Priest and radiates with the glory of God (1:9-20). Among those worshiping are 144,000 from every tribe in Israel and countless numbers from other nations (7:1-17). There are 144,000 virginal men (14:1-5) who accompany Jesus, the Lamb of God who opens the divine secrets to those who share in the heavenly liturgy (5:6-14). The altar in heaven is built over the bones of the martyrs who cry out from beneath the altar (6:9-11), "How long will it be, O Master, holy and true, before you judge our cause and avenge our blood among the inhabitants of the earth?" Catholics take it quite literally that the Liturgy of the Eucharist is the enactment of these heavenly realities. Even their altars by tradition are built over the tombs of martyrs or have pieces of their bones imbedded in the table. At the end of the book, the Church in the image of a Bride cries out with the Spirit of God, "Come, Lord Jesus!" The liturgy in Revelations is the pattern for the earthly Eucharistic Liturgy in which the saints worship God and the Lamb who was slain. The book ends with a cry that the Lord who was dead but now reigns alive would come again; this very proclamation of faith the Church has placed at the center of its Eucharistic Prayer.

The Church's liturgy teaches the Communion of Saints. Faith in the Communion of Saints is enshrined in the Apostle's Creed used by candidates at baptism to proclaim their faith in union with the whole Church. In the Liturgy, prayers are offered for all the members of the Church, living and dead, for all are alive to the Lord. Prayers are also offered to the deceased saints who are recognized for their sanctity on earth, and Catholics believe are already admitted to the liturgy in heaven. By tradition, these prayers are particularly directed to the martyrs who join Christ in his sacrifice by shedding their own blood. What happens to the members happens to the Head, the persecution of his members is the persecution of Christ. What the martyrs received in the Eucharist on earth they return to God as they enter heaven, the blood of his Son. Honor given to the martyrs is honor given to Christ whom they honor by their death. That is why the altar which represents Christ in the midst of his people also by tradition holds the bones of the martyrs. Other saints are also honored in the liturgy, especially John the Baptist, the Apostles and other disciples of Jesus. The most prominent of all the saints is Mary the Theotokos, the God-Bearer, who gave the world its Savior. The Church's liturgy is a primer on its faith in the communio it shares in Christ.

Mary

Anselm (d. 1109) taught that by God's design all creation owes as much to Mary as to God. God created the universe but would not recreate it except Mary gave her consent to be the mother of God's Son. Mary, a member of the Church, was the Mother of the world re-created through her Son, Jesus Christ. This faith of the Church attained its zenith in the west during the high Middle Ages but was prominent in the east from the first centuries. The early Councils of the Church, held in the east, vied to honor the Mother of God. The eastern liturgies repeatedly invoked the prayers of Mary. This Catholic sense of the preeminent place of Mary in salvation history and in the prayer of the Church was shared by all Christian Churches prior to the Protestant Reformation. The Church's declaration of Mary's perpetual virginity also had its roots in the liturgy. It mirrored the Church's self-understanding.

The Church is the Bride of Christ. Though composed of sinners it is made holy by Christ who cleanses it, washing it in his own blood. Unfaithful to God and being themselves sinners, the members of the Church are made virginal and holy by the same Spirit that overshadowed Mary. Virginity is best understood as the inability to fulfill ones own hopes and destiny, until God who makes one fruitful finds a home in you. Mary's perpetual virginity and the Church's holiness declare that the work of God in both of them can only be fulfilled by God in heaven. Indeed, as the Church celebrates the saints in glory it has, by tradition in both the east and the west, honored Mary as already assumed by God's power body and soul into heaven. The Church honors Mary above all the other saints because without her "Yes" to God none could share in the holiness of God, which she shares now in all its fullness.

The Church also honors Mary as Christ's first and faithful disciple. Mary is said to have conceived Christ in her soul by faith in God's word to her, before she conceived the word in her womb by the Spirit's power. The faith of Mary is evidence that the Spirit prepared her beforehand to be the Mother of God. This prior preparation is called the Immaculate Conception of Mary. The Catholic Church teaches that Mary was conceived in her mother's womb without sin. This is a grace of God given her in virtue of the suffering and death of Christ whom she would bear. Gabriel, in announcing the plan of God, refers to this predestination of Mary. The angel addresses Mary (Luke 1:28) as "full of grace" or "highly favored daughter" who is "blessed among women." Christian saints and scholars contemplating the few Scriptural references to Mary consistently speak of the great mystery of her holiness manifest in such simplicity that Martin Luther could declare, "She did only what was in her to do." This is the essence of Catholic sainthood. A saint is God's essay on what it means to be Christ in a particular time, place, and circumstance. A saint does only what is in her or him, but by God's grace it is more than one can accomplish alone. Mary gave birth to Christ, accompanied him on his earthly journey, and gathered with his disciples after the Resurrection. She is the Church's primary witness to what it means to bring forth Christ in one's own life. Jesus declares (Mark 3:34-35) that his brothers, sisters and mother are those who hear the word of God and keep it. In doing so he declares the glory of Mary but also opens the way for all to be saints. Sanctity is the work of God's Spirit in the believer, bringing forth from his or her life the presence of Christ in the world.

Intercessory Prayer

The prayer of a just person finds favor with God. This is the faith of Israel of old. The New Israel of God, the Church, also believes that the prayers of the saints find favor with God. The Apostles repeatedly encouraged Christians to pray for each other. The prayers of the Apostles brought healing to many. This tradition of intercessory prayer has not ceased in the Church. Catholics believe that all the saints, in heaven and on earth, intercede for each other and for the world. The Protestant reformers rejected the notion that the dead could intercede for the living or the living for the dead. They did so in part because Catholic piety presented the saints in heaven as mediators between the living and God. This Protestant rejection occurred in part because of the culture of the Middle Ages. The Catholic faith could not escape the emphatic emphasis on hierarchy in feudal societies. One could not go over the head of one's immediate patron. If Mary, an Apostle, or some other saint was the patron of one's local community or trade, it was proper to ask that saint's intercession. Going straight to Christ or the Father would have been a breach of social etiquette and so of piety. Obviously, the more correct understanding of Catholic Faith is that the intercession of the saints is an expression of *communio* among the believers and therefore of the life of the Trinity shared among them. There can be no prayer that is not directed to God, even as it seeks community support whether from the saints on earth or those in heaven. All prayer to the saints is prayer directed to God within the community of faith.

The patronage of the saints is also a Catholic tradition. The early Churches claimed as their founders and patrons various Apostles or Evangelists. Mary, the Mother of God, was obviously the patroness of the whole Church of God since she was the mother of its Head. Christians at baptism or confirmation took the names of saints. Those entering religious communities chose a saint's name to signal a complete conversion of life and the desire to emulate the saint's virtues or holiness. Saintly patronage was a way of establishing a rather permanent community bond with those who had lived the Gospel life and now were believed to have inherited its promises.

Canonization

Canonization is the process by which members of the Church are enrolled as approved saints whose patronage and intercession may be sought during liturgical or private prayer. Early Christian martyrs were honored in places where they were buried. There was not much official process necessary since many knew of the martyr's witness and veneration was spontaneous. By the fourth century, those called "confessors" were also declared saints. Confessors at first were those who had confessed their faith under persecution but had not suffered death. Later, confessors became a category filled by those whose lives confessed their faith in the Lord in a particularly profound way. Great pastors and women vowed to virginity were also canonized. During the first millennium, canonization took place in local Churches. Diocesan bishops approved honors given to persons who had lived in their local Church and whom after death the faithful venerated. In the late 900s, the first canonization took place at Rome. By the 1200s, the centralization of Papal authority led to laws stipulating all canonizations be approved by Rome. It was not until the eighteenth century that the current process was outlined. It has been revised several times since, the latest being approved by John Paul II (d. 2005).

The process for canonization is now introduced in the diocese of the deceased where the initial investigation occurs. That is followed by an appeal to Rome to accept the "cause." The person is enrolled as "Servant of God." The investigation of the person's sanctity and orthodoxy continues. During this time a "promoter" of the cause guides the investigation which is reviewed by another official, who used to be called a "devil's advocate," for doubts and objections. Following these investigations, the person may be enrolled as "Blessed" in the liturgical calendar. Essential for this elevation is either martyrdom or some miracle, usually a healing of a bodily ailment through the intercession of the proposed saint and without any other scientifically discernable cause. With further investigation and another miraculous healing, the blessed may be canonized as a saint. Canonization ceremonies for sainthood are presided over by the Pope.

Confusing Language and Concepts

Language about the veneration of Mary and the saints has been confusing. It was not unusual in the nineteenth and early twentieth century to speak of "worshiping" Mary. The use of this term for devotion to Mary was an extension of the romantic culture popular in Europe at the time. "Worship" was often used in literature to describe deeply emotional relationships. It should be clear to the reader that "worship" in Catholic Tradition is a theological term properly directed only to God. However, cultural accretions like this have confused the veneration of Mary and the saints with the worship of God. The Magisterium has repeatedly clarified the difference, but cultural forces regularly obscure the distinction. This has been the case particularly among newly evangelized peoples whose native religion included a pantheon of gods under a chief deity. That kind of world-view is reminiscent of

European feudalism's system of governance. Ongoing catechesis is necessary to counter these misconceptions of Catholic faith and practice. Catholic art has helped. The Last Judgment by Michaelangelo which graces the Vatican's Sistine Chapel depicts Christ as the one who directs the judgment of God. He is the powerful center and mediator of the consummation of God's saving work. The saints, including Mary, participate in the glory that is his but do not themselves accomplish it. Christ who shares their humanity is the center and cause of their *communio* with God whose holiness he bestows upon the saints.

Any discussion of canonized saints raises questions concerning what Catholics believe happens after death. The Protestant reformers, reacting to culturally confusing language and images, held that only what happens prior to death affected a person's salvation. Prayers for the dead had no effect, and the saints in heaven could not affect the Church on earth. The Catholic understanding of the Communion of Saints allows for the intercession of the saints but also for intercession for the sake of the dead. The Catholic world-view is that all, living and dead, are alive to God and remain in the *communio* of the Trinitarian life. This still does not answer the question of what happens after death. Is there any time after death or does time collapse in eternity? Can one speak of a period of time after death until the last judgment and the resurrection of the body? Are there other things, like the currently popular notion of "the rapture," that will happen "in the meantime?" The generally accepted answer is that no one knows for certain. What Catholics believe is that accepting or rejecting God's grace in this life already brings judgment. The judgment of God has been rendered in Christ and is salvation. However, salvation must be accepted by faith. God already reigns in the world through the Church and will send Christ to bring about the fulfillment of judgment and salvation at a time known only to God. At that time Christ will make all human intentions known and bring to completion the judgment of God. There is a hell and the possibility of damnation but not a certainty as to whom among humankind, if anyone, will be damned. There is certainty about the Kingdom of Heaven being revealed in all its fullness and that many will be glorified with Christ, sharing in their own humanity what is proper to them as adopted sons and daughters of God.

What happens until the Second Coming to those who have died? Are they in heaven or hell already? It was popular in the past to speak of a particular judgment of the soul at death and its immediate assignment to heaven, hell or purgatory. Purgatory in popular thought was a period of time to make up for punishment due to sin. After satisfaction was made, the soul would then enter heaven. All the souls would be joined to risen bodies at the Second Coming of Christ and then each person assigned to heaven or hell at the final judgment. As is evident from the treatment of Purgatory in chapter 6, this kind of popular imagery does not do justice to the Church's faith. The faith of the Church is there can be no certainty about how eternity will unfold as long as we live within the boundary of time. What faith does give is certitude that God who began the good work in the saints will bring it to completion on the last day in the communion with the Blessed Trinity. Until God is all in all, the saints intercede for one another as the Spirit wills in the communion of the Church.

Women

This book begins with the observation that diversity among the first disciples of Jesus was an early mark of the catholicity or universality of the Church. The book now comes to its conclusion with a reflection on the inclusion of women in the Communion of Saints. Currently, the Catholic Church is not looked upon as a leader in including women. Over the last century, women in western societies have steadily gained greater civil rights and secured protections for their dignity as persons. These civil advancements for women in developed nations have few obvious parallels in the structures of the Catholic Church. The Church is often faulted for not including women in more substantial leadership roles, especially in ordination as bishops, priests or deacons. What the Catholic Church has done consistently is include women in its communion of life. For example, in a centuries-old nuptial blessing, the groom was reminded that his bride is his equal to the life of grace. Women over the Christian centuries founded hundreds of religious orders whose members advanced education, science, social welfare and medical care not only in the Church but in societies all around the world. Without women the missionary and educational efforts of the Church could not have been accomplished over the last two hundred years. Today women are being appointed to major leadership roles in diocesan curias. Nevertheless, the inclusion of women in the Church has never been principally hierarchical but always strikingly charismatic.

Like the gift Jesus bestowed upon Mary of Magdala, that she would be the apostle to the Apostles and announce his resurrection, the Spirit has bestowed upon countless women in the Church extraordinary gifts of holiness and spiritual leadership. Beginning in the New Testament, women cared for the needs of Jesus and his Apostles and women stood with him at the cross while the Apostles fled. Women received Paul into their homes and helped his missionary effort through their business income. Great women saints and mystics have left their mark through the centuries. Julian of Norwich (d. 1413) was an anchoress, a female hermit who lived for over twenty years in a walled-in space attached to an English parish church. She left a record of her visions and meditations that after seven hundred years remains a spiritual classic. In addition to the service of prayer that anchoresses like Julian offered the Church, women who were reformed prostitutes, known as Magdalenes, gathered together in common lives of prayer, penitence, and mutual protection. Beguines were women who lived in communes for mutual support but who held private property and could leave to marry. Their ministry was to the poor and to mystical prayer. One of their number, Mechtild of Magdeburg (c. 1294), produced works of music and mystical poetry in the thirteenth century whose depth has moved many to a new appreciation of God's unity with all creation. St. Hildegard of Bingen (d. 1179) was a Benedictine Abbess who produced both scientific and theological works. Her prophecies in response to the corruption of her times earned her the title "the Sybil of the Rhine." Hildegard corresponded with Christian rulers and monks who sought her advice. St. Catherine of Sienna's (d. 1388) correspondence with popes was instrumental in the return of the Papacy to Rome after its seventy years at Avignon in France. Her spiritual diary earned her the title, Doctor of the Church. Catherine was attached to a lay society of Dominicans. Two Carmelite nuns, St. Teresa of Avila (d. 1582) and St. Therese of Lisieux, the Little Flower, (d. 1897) are also called Doctors of the Church because of their spiritual diaries. The spiritual testaments of these three women are held by the Church to be among the most profound spiritual insights of the Catholic Tradition. They join Mary of Magdala in announcing the work of God to ordained and lay alike.

Countless other examples may be given of women who have assured themselves a place among the charismatic leaders in the history of the Church. These few are given here to indicate that the place of women in the Church is not a matter of hierarchical structure but of charismatic spiritual gifts. Indeed, if women ever are ordained again as deaconesses or if by some work of the Spirit they are given any other share in the sacrament of Holy Orders, no such structural change will add anything to the share they already have in the *communio* of the Church. The share women and men have in the Trinitarian life is not measured by hierarchical structures but is a gift given in full measure to each member by the Spirit. The call to holiness is universal in the Catholic Church, as are the means for the complete transformation of every person into the divine likeness.

Appendix

The Sign of the Cross
In the name of the Father and of the Son and of the Holy Spirit. Amen.

The Our Father
Our Father who are in heaven, hallowed be your name. Your kingdom come, your will be done on earth as it is in heaven. Give us this day our daily bread and forgive us our trespasses as we forgive those who trespass against us and lead us not into temptation but deliver us from evil. (For the kingdom and the power and the glory are yours now and forever.) Amen.

The Jesus Prayer
Lord Jesus Christ, Son of God, have mercy on me a sinner.

The Hail Mary
Hail Mary full of grace, the Lord is with you. Blessed

are you among women and blessed is the fruit of your womb, Jesus. Holy Mary, Mother of God, pray for us sinners now and at the hour of our death. Amen.

The Doxology
Glory be to the Father and to the Son and to the Holy Spirit, as it was in the beginning is now and will be forever. Amen

The Glory to God (Gloria)
Glory to God in the highest,
  and peace to his people on earth.
Lord God, heavenly King,
almighty God and Father,
  we worship you, we give you thanks,
  we praise you for your glory.
Lord Jesus Christ, only Son of the Father,
Lord God, Lamb of God,
you take away the sin of the world:
  have mercy on us;
you are seated at the right hand of the Father:
  receive our prayer.
For you alone are the Holy One,
you alone are the Lord,
you alone are the Most High,
  Jesus Christ,
  with the Holy Spirit,
  in the glory of God the Father.
  Amen.

Eucharistic Prayer II

Presider: The Lord be with you.
Assembly: And also with you.
Presider: Lift up your hearts.
Assembly: We lift them up to the Lord.
Presider: Let us give thanks to the Lord our God.
Assembly: It is right to give him thanks and praise.

Presider:
Father, it is our duty and our salvation, always and everywhere
to give you thanks through your beloved Son, Jesus Christ.
He is the Word through whom you made the universe, the Savior you sent to redeem us.
By the power of the Holy Spirit he took flesh and was born of the Virgin Mary.
For our sake he opened his arms on the cross;
he put an end to death and revealed the resurrection.
In this he fulfilled your will and won for you a holy people.
And so we join the angels and the saints in proclaiming your glory as we say/sing:
Assembly:
Holy, holy, holy Lord, God of power, God of might.
Heaven and earth are full of your glory. Hosanna in the highest!
Blessed is he that comes in the name of the Lord. Hosanna in the highest!

Presider:
Lord, you are holy indeed, the fountain of all holiness.
Let your Spirit come upon these gifts to make them holy,
so that they may become for us the body + and blood of our Lord, Jesus Christ.
Before he was given up to death, a death he freely accepted,
he took bread and gave you thanks.
He broke the bread, gave it to his disciples, and said:
Take this, all of you, and eat it:
this is my body which will be given up for you.
When supper was ended, he took the cup.
Again he gave you thanks and praise, gave the cup to his disciples, and said:
Take this, all of you, and drink from it:
this is the cup of my blood, the blood of the new and everlasting covenant.
It will be shed for you and for all so that sins may be forgiven. Do this in memory of me.
Let us proclaim the mystery of faith:

Assembly:
Christ has died, Christ is risen, Christ will come again.

Presider:
In memory of his death and resurrection, we offer you, Father,
this life-giving bread, this saving cup.

We thank you for counting us worthy to stand in your presence and serve you.

May all of us who share in the body and blood of Christ be brought together in unity by the Holy Spirit.

Lord, remember your Church throughout the world: make us grow in love,

together with _____ our Pope, _____ our bishop, and all the clergy.

Remember our brothers and sisters who have gone to their rest

in the hope of rising again; bring them and all the departed into the light of your presence.

Have mercy on us all: make us worthy to share eternal life

with Mary, the virgin Mother of God, with the apostles, and with all the saints

who have done your will throughout the ages.

May we praise you in union with them, and give you glory,

through your Son, Jesus Christ.

Through him, with him, in him, in the unity of the Holy Spirit,

all glory and honor is yours, almighty Father, for ever and ever.

Assembly:
Amen!

Bibliography

For a more comprehensive study of the teachings of the Catholic Church consult the *Catechism of the Catholic Church*, 2nd Edition (Liberia Editrice Vaticana, 2000), or the *Compendium of the Catechism of the Catholic Church*, or the *United States Catholic Catechism for Adults*.

If the reader is interested in a simple explanation of the formulation both of the Bible and of Catholic theology see *The College Student's Introduction to Theology*, Thomas P. Rausch, Ed. (The Liturgical Press, Collegeville, MN, 1993).

The Liturgy of the Hours is available from various publishers in a complete four volume set or in a simplified single volume version containing Morning, Evening and Night Prayer. Ask at any book store which specializes in Catholic literature.

An easy-to-read explanation of Catholic practices is available in the revised and updated *Catholic Customs and*

Traditions: A Popular Guide, Greg Dues (Twenty-Third Publications, Mystic, CT, 2003)

For those interested in a practical guide to the appreciation of the liturgical seasons and their celebration in a parish community see *To Crown the Year* (Liturgical Training Publications, Chicago, IL, 1995).